Twayne's United States Authors Series

Sylvia E. Bowman, *Editor*

INDIANA UNIVERSITY

James Purdy

TUSAS 248

*Photo by Fabian Bachrach, courtesy
of Farrar, Straus and Cudahy*

James Purdy

JAMES PURDY

By HENRY CHUPACK

*Kingsborough Community College of
The City University of New York*

TWAYNE PUBLISHERS
A DIVISION OF G. K. HALL & CO., BOSTON

Library of Congress Cataloging in Publication Data

Chupack, Henry.
  James Purdy.

  (Twayne's United States authors series; TUSAS 248)
  Bibliography: p. 137–41.
  Includes index.
  1. Purdy, James—Criticism and interpretation.
PS3531.U426Z67   813'.5'4   74-22438
ISBN 0-8057-0601-1

To Leah Again with Love

Contents

About the Author

Henry Chupack is Professor of English at Kingsborough Community of the City University of New York. He has previously served as Chairman of the Division of Language, Literature and the Arts of that institution. Born and reared in New York, Dr. Chupack received his A.B. from Brooklyn College and his Ph.D. (1952) from New York University. He has held teaching positions at Brooklyn College, C. W. Post College of Long Island University, and the New York Institute of Technology, where he served as chairman of the English Department.

A specialist in American literature and the American novel, Dr. Chupack is the author of *Roger Williams* for the Twayne United States Authors Series (1969). He has also written articles on Walt Whitman, whose last years in Camden furnished the subject for his doctoral dissertation. He is currently involved in a study tentatively entitled "The American Novel in the Seventies."

Preface

Never have the qualities and attributes of good writing such as boldness, vigor, immediacy, directness, and diversity been more evident in the creation of American fiction than in the three decades since the end of World War II. This great efflorescence in technique and artistry has probably been due in great measure to the need of postwar writers to record and describe in new and hitherto untold ways the many changes and dislocations wrought in our way of life as a result of our highly evolved technological society.

In the three decades since Pearl Harbor, the nature of American society has been so transformed from what it was in the 1920s and 1930s as to make such terms as *flaming youth, Babbitt, Okies,* and *proletarian literature* serve as little more than footnotes to a bygone era. In the meantime, our society has moved relentlessly and dynamically forward, caught up in the swirling political, economic, and racial currents of our own times. We have only to compare the fiction of the 1920s and the 1930s with that of the 1970s to realize these differences. In the decade following World War I the activities and antics of the members of the Lost Generation served as major themes for F. Scott Fitzgerald and Ernest Hemingway. In the 1930s, John Dos Passos, James Farrell, and John Steinbeck were able practitioners of what came to be regarded as radical or proletarian fiction, interested as they were in the lives of those uprooted and dispossessed by the 1929 Depression.

In our own day, two of the more significant themes reflecting the turbulent changes which have been pursued by the talented writers of the last three decades have been the absurdity of life and society on the one hand and the mental aberrations and abnormalities of the individual on the other. These themes are not new to us, thanks to such early writers as Edgar Allan Poe and Nathaniel Hawthorne, and to William Faulkner in our time;

but such subjects prevail today. We have only to read through the fiction of contemporary authors of such disparate backgrounds as John Barth, Joseph Heller, Thomas Pynchon, Vladimir Nabokov, Bruce Jay Friedman, Walker Percy, and Irvin Faust—to mention just a few—to realize how nearly all of their important novels and short stories, such as *Giles Goat-Boy, Catch-22, V., Pale Fire, Stern, The Moviegoer,* and *Roar, Lion, Roar* are literally caught up in miasmic proportions with either the madness of American life or the alienation of the individual; in some cases, they deal with both phenomena. We have merely to think of Captain Yossarian in *Catch-22* to realize how, in an insane military world, Yossarian, the one indestructibly sane person, is regarded as mad simply because he refuses to accept the values of his peers and superiors.

In mentioning these themes as two of the more important ones of current fiction, we must necessarily include the works of those contemporary Southern writers whose fictional creations of the emotionally ill and mentally maimed have shown the extent to which the Gothic imagination has illuminated, as it were, the haunted house of the mind. Among these writers, Carson McCullers, Truman Capote, Flannery O'Connor, and Eudora Welty immediately come to mind as a few of the more recent practitioners of what has been termed the *new American Gothic.* A writer usually linked with them is James Purdy, who, though not of Southern background, has employed Gothic devices, especially in his early fiction, to very good effect.

In addition to being a startling original limner of the grotesque and the emotionally disabled, Purdy, like Welty and McCullers, is also a satirist and a black humorist, whose stories and novels, particularly *Cabot Wright Begins* have weighed many aspects of modern American life and found them absurd, wanting at best, or—at worst—terrifying in its lack of concern for the individual.

Thus Purdy, like other important contemporary writers, unites in his fiction two of the foremost themes of the day. Yet Purdy is far from being accepted as a major writer; his fiction, since its first publication in the late 1950s and to date, in the early 1970s, has received a mixed reception from literary critics and reviewers. The late Dame Edith Sitwell, for example, one of Purdy's adulators, regarded him as a "very considerable novelist and short-story writer . . . in the very highest rank of contemporary writers."[1] However, another also deceased critic, Stanley Edgar Hyman, found him to be "a terrible writer and worse than that . . . a boring writer."[2]

Still, in light of the rating given him in the Book Week section of September 26, 1965, of the now defunct *New York Herald Tribune*, which was concerned with the quality of American fiction since the end of World War II, Purdy's literary reputation ranked higher than his detractors recognized. He was not listed among the first twenty authors who had "written the most distinguished fiction" during the last generation, but he was in the next five, grouped with Mary McCarthy, Philip Roth, James Gould Cozzens, and the late John Steinbeck. To be ranked with Steinbeck and Cozzens, both of whom had been writing much longer than Purdy, must be viewed as a real tribute to him; for, at the time, he had published only some two dozen short stories and three novels.

In 1963, as if to presage Purdy's inclusion among America's first twenty-five writers of "distinguished fiction," in *The Creative Present: Notes on Contemporary American Fiction*, editors Nona Balakian and Charles Simmons indicated that, had the original plan of the book not been limited to ten essays evaluating the work of seventeen leading American writers of the postwar generation, Purdy, as well as Flannery O'Connor, would have been the two fictionists discussed in the eleventh essay. Therefore, if for no other reason than to assess rightly the output of an author who is highly regarded in some literary circles—but whose fiction at its best has yet not attained the popularity of Bernard Malamud's, Saul Bellow's, and Philip Roth's, for example—a study of Purdy is necessary.

This book attempts to fulfill the need for such a work. Accordingly, the seven chapters of this study are devoted to separate analyses of Purdy's fiction. Chapters 2 through 4 are devoted to an analytical study of the early short stories and longer fiction, such as *Color of Darkness*, *Malcolm*, *The Nephew*, and *Children Is All*; the latest three novels, *Cabot Wright Begins*, *Eustace Chisholm and The Works*, and *Jeremy's Version* constitute the subject matter for chapters 5 and 6; and chapter 7 will assess Purdy's place in contemporary American fiction. The first chapter introduces the pertinents facts of Purdy's life, the major themes pervading his fiction, and related literary matters.

As has been indicated, Purdy has not been so widely read as some of his more popular contemporaries. I have therefore taken the position that, aside from *Malcolm*, his most popular novel, many readers may not be acquainted with Purdy's other works; consequently, for each story and novel, I have summarized and included only so much of the plot as to make intelligible the comments and analyses that follow. Too, wherever applicable, I have included excerpts of reviews that denote the mixed attitudes that Purdy's work has consistently received.

Giving added piquancy to this study is the fact that, although it is the first full-length analysis of his fiction, James Purdy is not happy with the fact that this book is being written. I first spoke to Purdy in January, 1966, a particularly bad time, as I remember, since *Malcolm*, which had recently been transformed into a play by Edward Albee, had been given poor reviews and had closed some ten days after it opened. Only later did I learn how deeply Purdy abhorred certain literary and drama critics. I believe the poor reception given Albee's adaptation of the novel only helped to make him hostile to anyone or anything which would expose him to the public as my proposed study of his fiction would. With this attitude of the subject author understood, it is hoped that, as a result of this study, serious readers and students of contemporary American fiction will be introduced to one of the more interesting, if not exactly popular, writers of our day.

HENRY CHUPACK

Kingsborough Community College of
The City University of New York

Acknowledgments

I gratefully acknowledge the permission of Farrar, Straus and Giroux to quote excerpts from *Malcolm, The Nephew, Cabot Wright Begins,* and *Eustace Chisholm and The Works*. Doubleday and Company must also be thanked for granting me permission to quote several short passages from *Jeremy's Version*.

Chronology

1923   James Purdy born July 14, 1923, near Fremont, Ohio, the middle son of five boys of William and Vera (Covick) Purdy.

1926   Parents divorced; early years spent in straitened circumstances.

1936–   Attended various high schools in Ohio; encouraged by
1940   one of his English teachers to become a writer.

1940   Graduated from a high school in Chicago.

1941   Attended the University of Chicago.

1943   Began writing fiction; some of his early stories were accepted by *Evergreen Review, Creative Writing,* and *Mademoiselle.*

1946   Attended graduate courses at University of Chicago.

1946–   Traveled to Latin America, France, and Spain.
1948

1949   Became a member of the faculty at Lawrence College, Wisconsin.

1953   Left Lawrence College to become a full-time writer.

1955   Association with Osborn Andreas and Dr. J. J. Sjoblom resulted in private publication of *63: Dream Palace.*

1956   *63: Dream Palace* published in England.

1957   Publication of *63: Dream Palace* in America by New Directions Press.

1959   *Malcolm.*

1960   *The Nephew.*

1961   *Children Is All.*

1964   *Cabot Wright Begins.*

1967   *Eustace Chisholm and The Works.*

1970   *Jeremy's Version.*

CHAPTER 1

The Loveless World of James Purdy

I The Purdian Trauma

JAMES Purdy's unsuccessful efforts to get his early fiction
published in America is a well-known fact in the literary
circles of New York.[1] As late as 1966 he could still say, "My
struggle in America to get published has been such a traumatic
shock that I can never forgive anybody who put me through
it. . . ."[2] Purdy's self-admission of the psychic toll which the
nonpublication of his early fiction still exacts from him is significant. To him, it makes no difference that his early rejected
fiction was published in England a decade earlier, in 1956, under
the title of *63: Dream Palace*, where it drew highly laudatory
reviews, which led to the publication of the work in America
a year later; or that, since 1956, all his later fiction, both short
stories and novels, as well as his plays, have been published by
such American publishers as Farrar, Straus, Giroux and, later,
by Doubleday. In fact, ten years of fairly successful writing
have not eliminated the "traumatic shock" of his early frustration.

Additional evidence of the searing effect that this early lack
of recognition had upon Purdy, who "wanted to be a writer
from earliest memory," is his admission that "he has little faith
in reviewers, very little faith in the general public, and altogether
none in regard to publishers," since all three categories "have
seldom been interested in writing or the truth."[3] Accepting
his statement at face value, we wonder why Purdy has bothered
to write at all, and why he is this negative despite the fair, and
in some cases, almost adulatory, reviews his early fiction has
received. Moreover, his assertion that all three categories "have
seldom been interested in writing or the truth" is too preposterous
to be taken seriously; it must be seen for what it is—the extremely
negative reaction of one who must literally have suffered the

tortures of the damned in his attempt to establish himself as a literary artist.

The traumatic shock occasioned by the nonpublication of his early fiction and his adverse opinion of people who publish, review, or read books are, however, not the sum total of Purdy's animadversions. For example, we have his statement about American life: "American civilization [is] a totalitarian machine, very similar to Russia's . . . the only way to cope with it is to ignore it as much as possible."[4] To ignore what he considers evil in the hope that it will leave by itself is an ostrichlike attitude unworthy of an intelligent adult; but this remark must be viewed as the outburst of a man who has apparently been so deeply hurt by certain aspects of American life as to wish to be undisturbed by the responsibilities of living in a political and social context. In addition to these negative admissions by Purdy, two other factors must be considered in any evaluation of his fiction: the formative years of his life and the facts behind the initial nonpublication of his early work in the United States.

II   *The Matrix of a Writer*

Purdy has allowed very few facts of his life to become known, and those that are available help prepare readers to understand some of the hardships he must have experienced as a writer; they also serve to reinforce the impression that his early years may have been somewhat similar to those experienced by many of the children in his stories, who almost always suffer from their relationships with adults—and most of all from those with their parents.

Born near Fremont, Ohio, on July 14, 1923, the son of William and Vera (Covick) Purdy, both Scotch-English Presbyterians, young James, the middle child in a family of five boys, soon became, like some of the blighted children in his tales, a child of divorced parents. His early years were spent in severe circumstances, and he grew up spending much of his time traveling and attending many high schools in his native state; eventually he was graduated from a high school in Chicago, the city where he found many of the fascinating characters who later appear in his fiction. And much like two famous Midwestern writers before him—Theodore Dreiser and Carl Sandburg—young Purdy was encouraged by one of his English teachers to become a writer. Though he never enjoyed school, this encouragement led him to make writing his "real life" and to regard all future work and tasks unrelated to it as onerous.

After graduation from high school, Purdy attended first the University of Chicago and later the University of Puebla in Mexico, where he learned Spanish. This language helped him to obtain a position in Havana, Cuba, in a private boys' school, where he taught English. Later, he returned to the United States and took graduate courses at the University of Chicago. Still later he studied at the University of Madrid. Thanks to his ability as a linguist, he was able to earn his travel expenses for various trips he made to Latin America, France, and Spain. In addition to his knowledge of the Romance languages, Purdy could also read Latin and Greek, a practice he engages in daily when not writing. In 1949, at the age of twenty-six, Purdy became a member of the faculty at Lawrence College in Wisconsin, where, after four years, he quit teaching and what he termed the "dead air of the suburbs" to become a full-time writer.

Purdy has written fiction since he was twenty, and some of his stories have been published by such magazines as *Evergreen Review*, *Creative Writing*, and *Mademoiselle*. In the early 1950s he assembled a batch of his stories and sent them to front-rank publishers; rejection slips were all he received in return, some of them caustic. The *New Yorker* magazine, for example, told him he had "no talent whatsoever." These hostile receptions and experiences with critics and publishers later figure in the plot of *Cabot Wright Begins*, in which currently renowned book reviewers and publishers are scathingly portrayed.

In 1955, Osborn Andreas, an American businessman whose literary bent resulted in a study of Henry James, read Purdy's rejected tales and decided they merited a private printing. In the same year Dr. J. J. Sjoblom, a young, impoverished chemist, borrowed money at great expense to have Purdy's novella *63: Dream Palace* published privately; and what followed is now literary history. With a thousand copies of the stories available for distribution, Andreas encouraged Purdy to send copies to

those writers and critics he most admired, most of whom were
English, and all of whom reacted with enthusiasm to Purdy's
tales. Thrilled with this reception, Purdy then sent a copy of
63: Dream Palace to Dame Edith Sitwell, who was as impressed
with the novella as she had been by the tales. Until her death, in
1961, she encouraged Purdy to continue writing. Thanks to her
efforts, all of these early stories and the novella were published
under the same title by an English publisher in 1956; a year
later *New Directions Press*, which for the previous ten years
had constantly rejected all of Purdy's manuscripts, became his
first American publisher, publishing the stories and novella
under the title of *Color of Darkness*.

The first important American writer to be impressed with
Purdy's writing was Carl Van Vechten, the late Negro novelist,
who had the young writer meet him in New York and who
encouraged him to persevere in his chosen career. Thanks to
Van Vechten's good offices, Purdy's early unpublished manuscripts and revisions were placed in the care of the Yale University Library. And, while he has finally managed, since 1957,
to have his work published in his native land, Purdy had no
illusions about American publishers, whose operations he likens
to "a kind of boy-scout machinery" which is tremendously
"arbitrary in its rejection of anyone it has not elected."[5] What
is even worse, he feels, is that the literary establishment in New
York has not forgiven him for "having discovered himself," and
for having thus nullified its intention from the outset of putting
his literary career into limbo.

Of medium height and slender physique, Purdy at last report
was still living in a frame apartment house on Henry Street in
the Brooklyn Heights area of New York City. There, because
of grants from the Guggenheim and the Ford Foundations, the
generosity of friends, and the royalties from his books, he has
managed to persevere in his uphill battle to write as he is
impelled to write. Now fifty-one, he is so deeply committed to
his writing, we feel, that he will remain at his desk for the
remainder of his life, regardless of the income this work nets
him, which up to now has not been much. Although his books
have been translated into some twenty-five languages, including
Turkish and Chinese, his first and still most popular novel

Malcolm netted him only eight thousand dollars, although two hundred and fifty thousand copies in paperback have so far been sold.

III *The Mental Climate, Themes, and Craftsmanship of Purdy's Fiction*

In *Time to Murder and Create: The Contemporary Novel in Crisis,* John W. Aldridge, lamenting the lack of imagination in the depiction of modern life, asserts that "the imagination of the contemporary novel, particularly in America, has remained locked in certain stereotyped modes of perceiving and recording reality that it has inherited from the modern classic literary past, but that, as stereotypes, have now ceased to relate meaningfully to the reality of which we are, or ought to be, most intensely aware."[6] While this view may be ascribed to a good many of the writers of the contemporary scene, this stricture cannot be levied against Purdy. Whether tracing the mental processes of a rapist, describing the bitter quarrels between husbands and wives, or accounting for the conflicts between parents and children, Purdy has definitely been alert to the life of our times and to "the reality of which we are, or ought to be, most intensely aware," and his imagination has been anything but "locked in certain stereotyped modes of perceiving and recording reality." In an age in which much American fiction has been characterized by the merely odd and freakish, Purdy's most successful fiction has had as its subject the dark underside and interiors of the human soul—in short, the buried life or, in Poe's phrase, the soul's "ghoul-haunted woodland of Weir," the delineation of which, according to Richard Chase, has been an integral part of the American novel since James Fenimore Cooper's day.[7]

Because of Purdy's many incisive and horrifying portrayals of distraught states of mind, which are presented in new and startling ways, he fulfills Nathalie Sarraute's dictum that the function of modern fiction is "to express something as yet unsaid," and that only this expression will allow the "novel form to keep forever its initial impact, its strength and its freshness."[8] Making Miss Sarraute's point even more valid is that, unlike other

Black Humorists of the 1960s who have seriously attacked American institutions and values, such as Joseph Heller, John Barth, and James J. P. Donleavy, Purdy appears to have gone beyond these writers in the constant reiteration of his basic theme—that our society is essentially a loveless one in which no one cares for anyone else, with the attendant numbness, lack of feeling and absence of concern that all this implies. This coldness or this insensitivity seems to have been brought about by a world grown so technologically complex, so impersonal and so uncaring, that people have lost their spiritual identity, not knowing who or what they are; consequently, they are spiritually incapable of caring for or about one another.

This lovelessness is best portrayed in Purdy's treatment of family life, one of his basic themes, where, because of the absence of affection, husbands and wives, as well as their children, lead barren lives. These children, while growing up, usually suffer severely at the hands of their parents. And, as if to indicate that parenthood is but a physical fact, Purdy presents a number of youngsters, usually boys orphaned early in life, who are in quest of a father to whom they can truly feel spiritually allied. Thus, in the first four novels, all the major male characters are orphans in either their adolescent or early adult years who are searching for a father, as is particularly true in *Malcolm*. However, the children born to loveless couples are portrayed as being no better off than the orphaned ones. As for those couples whom Purdy portrays as childless—here in stark and sere fashion is shown a barrenness that has never permitted even the thought of having offspring.

However, because a world without love is either too difficult to live with or to live in, and because of the eternal need to gain some degree of love or affection, many of these blighted youngsters are driven to either rape or homosexuality—this is another of Purdy's recurring themes. And, while these two forms of sexual expression may not be palatable fare to the average reader, these acts are never injected extraneously into the novels. Instead, each time such sexual acts are engaged in, credible motivation is offered, and verisimilitude is obtained. In *Eustace Chisholm and The Works*, for example, a novel

given over almost entirely to the world of homosexuality,
Purdy achieves some of his finest writing to date.

To appreciate better the social and intellectual milieu from
which Purdy's fiction has emerged, we must remember that
he was only twenty-two when the first atomic bomb burst over
Hiroshima; and, like the rest of his generation, he spent his
mature years in a period of unparalleled prosperity in American
life. Yet for Purdy affluent America has still not made any
sizable advances in eliminating the pockets of poverty in the
cornucopia of modern America. And though Purdy is adept in
portraying lives from all ranges of society, he has a special
affinity for the poor. He excels in describing the abnormality
of character that poverty can bring in its wake. And, whether
chronicling in one case quirks of character in the husband whose
wife and son have left him because he is poverty-stricken; or
whether recording the mental woes of the suburban matron who
hates her grown son because his long hippy beard offends her
sense of newly arrived status and respectability, the lack of
love, in each case leads to the suffering that Purdy's characters
undergo. They are not cared for or loved by others; hence, their
forlornness and rejection lead to their loss of identity.

Like Hawthorne, Purdy is both a moralist and a psychologist,
a prober of the innermost recesses of the heart; and, more often
than not, he produces vignettes that have the same power of
blackness that characterizes Hawthorne's best allegories. For
example, we have the case of the father who is such a narcissist
that he cannot remember the color of his little boy's eyes. This
small deficiency is only indicative of the father's failure to
establish any kind of rapport with his child—a failure that finally
leads to a ferocious hostility between the two. In those few
cases in which individuals are depicted as caring to some extent
for one another, the atmosphere of Purdy's fictional world is
so weird and diabolical that, in one instance, an older brother
is impelled to kill his younger one because of the latter's
superior sense of values.

Many of Purdy's characters would easily subscribe to the
credo set forth by Matthew Arnold in "Dover Beach" that this
life possesses "neither joy, nor love, nor light, nor certitude,
nor peace, nor help for pain." Arnold alluded to an outer world

devastated by Darwin's evolutionary theories, which negated long-held biblical postulates holding man as the special creation of God; Purdy's characters, on the other hand, have no such religious dilemma to contend with. Because of Purdy's Naturalistic bent, his characters are portrayed as merely physical beings —as biological specimens with no roots in anything making for permanence. Thus they are shown inhabiting their own interior, Kafkaesque worlds in which psychological states, as well as human actions, are the results of material causes. And, because of their inability to express or to receive love, they act in a manner which can only be described as either eerie, bizarre, or grotesque. Alienated from a true sense of themselves, they are also alienated from others.

In short, because of the chaotic forces let loose in American life since the end of World War II, and because of the highly technological advances that have taken place, literature has become synonymous with energy, with change. As a result, human beings have been torn loose from their normal psychological and psychic moorings. In an attempt to find spiritual identity and love, many of Purdy's characters resort finally to criminal acts and to violent sexuality, usually rape. But, in presenting such characters, Purdy does so with the sense of freshness and strength previously alluded to by Miss Sarraute in her remarks about the novel. And, while these characters are set forth with their backgrounds and antecedent actions completely omitted, we are almost immediately engaged in their problems because of the bare but importunate facts given. Again, while many of these characters would appear to be Negroes because of certain nuances of character, they can also be viewed as men and women of any race who are baring their innermost selves in any kind of depersonalized society. This unusual approach to character portrayal—one in which a twentieth-century Everyman is depicted—accounts precisely for the freshness and strength of most of Purdy's fiction.

Furthermore, in a world where more and more writers have begun to write in as disorderly and as disjointedly a fashion as the world they observe represents, Purdy achieves some of his best results by writing in a spare, lean manner that reminds us of Somerset Maugham at his best. Again, like Willa Cather and

Katherine Anne Porter, two stylists who come to mind, Purdy
regards his art as a craftsman would; for his fiction has to be
put together in the conscious and critical manner that attains
his predetermined esthetic and thematic goals. Thus his un-
adorned, straightforward, objective style is simply a device to
throw his readers off guard. For, when least expected, below
the seemingly placid surfaces he presents, pits of hell and darkness suddenly yawn open that literally chill our blood. Yet the
shock derives not so much from the contents as it does from the
style. And so effortlessly is all this done that we might fail to
appreciate the amount of effort Purdy must have expended to
obtain these effects. All told, like the goddess in Greek mythology,
Purdy's style of shock appears to have emerged fully developed
from his head from the very beginning, and it has remained
constant throughout his fiction.

Yet to obtain his mentally icy climate, Purdy employs very
few literary devices; the *mot juste* appears to be his forte. A
highly individualistic writer, whose style is altogether his own,
Purdy has apparently been uninfluenced by any of his contemporaries. The one writer with whom Purdy can perhaps be
compared is J. D. Salinger; for they both use children and
adolescents quite often as the major characters in their fiction.
The two writers are also quite similar in their use of dialogue
and in their sparing use of descriptive passages. Purdy's use of
dialogue is in fact one of his strengths as a writer; for, like
Sinclair Lewis, he possesses an uncanny flair for the rhythms
and accents of American speech, and for re-creating the language
patterns that people use in talking to one another. Like Lewis
also, Purdy is particularly adept in reproducing the flat nasal
speech of Midwesterners. An example of this capability is
shown by an excerpt from *The Nephew*, one in which Boyd
Mason informs his sister Alma that, in working as a schoolteacher out of state, she has missed much of what now constitutes
the present: "You mentioned a bit further back how much was
going on in Rainbow now. It's not what's going on now you've
missed out on as what went on when you weren't here at all."[9]

In his first novel, *Malcolm*, Purdy has one of his characters,
Madame Girard, remark, "Texture is all, substance is nothing."
If by texture is meant the structural quality resulting from the

artist's blending of elements, this statement can summarize very
well nearly all of Purdy's fiction. For, as Gerald Weales has
perceptively noted, "At his weakest, Purdy's texture is only
mannerism and his revelations become banal or vaguely 'poetic'
in the ugly sense of the word. When he is more effective, his
arrested moments become vivid enough to suggest substance
or to hide its absence. At his best, texture and substance
become one."[10] In his shorter fiction, where he has the opportunity for greater emotional impact because of the entailed
brevity, Purdy succeeds more often in achieving this oneness
than he does in his novels, where the effect tends to be more
diffuse. So far, only in *The Nephew* and in *Jeremy's Version*
has this artistry been so carefully controlled as to manage the
perfect fusion of texture and substance.

CHAPTER 2

The Early Stories: Color of Darkness

FIRST published by Victor Gollancz in London in 1956 under the title of *63: Dream Palace*, the tales included in this volume were highly praised by such British writers and critics as Edith Sitwell, Angus Wilson, and John Cowper Powys. These stories, as we have noted, were reissued the following year in New York by New Directions Press under the new title of *Color of Darkness*. That the lavish praise given Purdy's first published work by his English critics was not unduly excessive was seen in the generally favorable press given the American edition. Horace Gregory, for example, admitted that he had given up hope that anyone during the Eisenhower years was writing prose; but he thought that Purdy's narratives were the only new, deeply moving stories written in this country in the 1950s. William Peden was so impressed that he remarked that "not since the early stories of Tennessee Williams and Angus Wilson has there been so disturbing a first volume of short fiction."[1] According to W. T. Scott, Purdy's was a "rich and passionate talent, already capable of memorable work, an excitement in new American writing."[2]

Yet, in reading these stories, we can easily understand the various reasons that typical American publishers may have entertained for having previously refused to print them and why such an astute critic as Malcolm Cowley objected to *63: Dream Palace* as "obscene."[3] The Eisenhower years exemplified an age of conformity, and such novels as J. D. Salinger's *The Catcher in the Rye* and Saul Bellow's *The Adventures of Augie March*, with their understandable if at times confused protagonists, served as the normal grist for the average reader's mill. Many publishers may have felt that Purdy's tales, often dealing as they did with grotesque characters in most unusual and

27

abnormal situations, would simply have been beyond the average reader's experience. However, by 1957, spurred by the success of the English edition, New Directions Press evidently thought the time was ripe for Purdy to be given to his fellow Americans; and this assessment was correct.

I *Cruelty to Children*

Consisting of eleven stories and the novella *63: Dream Palace*, more than half of the tales in *Color of Darkness* have as their basic theme a deep sense of incompatibility, either between children and their parents or between husbands and wives. When the failure "to connect" is between the parent and the offspring, the mother usually is the one with whom her child cannot relate compatibly; however, in the title story of the collection, "Color of Darkness,"[4] the father is the culprit. Ostensibly a successful man at his work, which means more to him than anything else in the world, the relationship of this parent to anyone else or to anything else but his work (which, ironically enough, we are not told the nature of) is practically nonexistent. So absorbed is this twenty-eight-year-old narcissist in his occupation that he is unable to remember the color of his son Baxter's eyes, even after Mrs. Zilkie, the housekeeper who is helping him rear the boy, reminds him that his son's eyes are as blue as seawater. Nor can he remember the color of the eyes of his wife, who had run away a few years previously, presumably to rid herself of a mate who, in addition to his monomania for work, had married her because, as he understood it, everybody at some time in life got married.

An additional illustration of the man's self-serving nature is seen in his admission that he can remember people and become interested in them only if he really cares to do so. When informed by Mrs. Zilkie that Baxter needs someone to play with, the father manages to become directly involved in buying a small dog for his son; but he does so only because the housekeeper is loath to tramp the hard pavements to help her master buy one. Once Baxter has the dog, the father retreats to his normal unconcern for others; his parental duty for his child's happiness has apparently been fulfilled. Later, Baxter, entreated by the housekeeper and his father to remove from his mouth the wedding ring that his father had previously left on the table, refuses; and, when his father squats on the floor to plead with him, Baxter remembers that this is the very first time he had ever seen his parent in a position that indicated that he wished to play with him.

The wedding ring apparently denotes the father's previous tie with humanity, so to speak; and, since that link is already broken, the father presumably desires its return as a symbol of his having once been a member of the human race. Though he is successful in having Baxter finally spew it forth, for his pains Baxter kicks him violently in the groin. The blow apparently symbolizes the boy's desire to destroy the physical organ that made possible his birth into a loveless world, just as his spewing forth the ring may denote his hatred and contempt for the loveless union which gave him life. Twisting in pain, the father can merely answer Mrs. Zilkie, who wishes to help him, by saying that "right now" he is not ready to receive help, the "right now" apparently indicating his present lack of perception and his own inability to accept a parent's responsibility. Thus, in a mere twelve pages, divided into some six or seven episodes that build on one another to mount to a dismaying climax of violence, hatred, and rejection, Purdy has created a small classic in which he unites language, theme, and mood.

Almost as excellent as "Color of Darkness" is "Why Can't They Tell You Why?,"[5] another tale in which a woebegone child is the luckless victim. This time, however, the parent is a mother named Ethel, who has little or no rapport with her young son Paul. A widow, her husband having died in World War I, Ethel is unhappy about having to care for her son after her hard day's work. Paul, who has been out of school for two months because of illness, spends most of his time either in poring over pictures of his dead father or in listening to his mother bemoaning her fate to a friend over the telephone. In a savage climax, the mother, who resents Paul's calling her "Mama Ethel," which she construes as indicating that she is growing old, furiously seizes the photographs from the boy and starts burning them in the basement furnace, all because Paul is unable to explain his almost monomaniacal preoccupation with them. As Ethel interprets it, Paul prefers a dead father over a living mother. The irony, of course, is that she has been a "dead" mother who has shown her son little or no affection; and this lack of love has created the boy's hunger for his father's image.

Unable to snatch all the photographs which the boy vigorously clutches to his breast, Ethel does manage to grab a batch which she throws into the fire. Turning to seize the rest, she stops short, horrified at the sight of something black that is gushing forth from the boy's mouth. In a literal sense, this black substance could denote some of the pictures Paul may have attempted to swallow to save from his mother's grasp; again, it could symbolize his heart's blood having turned black in tremendous hatred against his mother for having denied him his father's image, even in death. Again, in a mere six or seven pages, Purdy has written a masterpiece that depicts the plight of all unloved children. Like the father in "Color of Darkness," Ethel is simply too self-centered to really care for others, even her own child.

In Purdy's treatment of cruelty to children, we are reminded of Charles Dickens's powerful depictions of the almost virulent hostility shown youngsters in Victorian England; but, where the English novelist was rather sprawling in his descriptions and rather sentimental in his touch, Purdy manages his effects very economically and leaves almost no room for sentiment. In Purdy's tales, children are literally to be ignored by their parents; and, if they cannot be, they are to be subordinated as quickly as possible.

In another powerful narrative "Cutting Edge,"[6] no longer is it a child who cannot communicate with his mother; instead, the victim is a twenty-four-year-old artist, Bobby Zeller, from New York; his crime is the shaggy, hippy beard he wears on a visit to his parents, whose home is in Florida. There, like most of Purdy's married couples, they live in a state of lovelessness. A domineering woman who has kept both husband and son under her control throughout her married life, Mrs. Zeller is so greatly concerned with suburban propriety that she cannot comprehend or tolerate her son's unorthodox appearance. The beard, of course, is Bobby's first attempt to challenge her hitherto undisputed rule. A talk with his father, who has been asked by his wife to intervene in her behalf, serves only to reveal that Bobby has never meant anything to the man. Thus Bobby is alienated from both parents, and his attempts to communicate with them fail. He soon realizes that his parents, though now in their forties, "had learned nothing from life" and had stopped growing mentally and spiritually some twenty years previously. Bobby remembers a maid his parents had hired when he was a mere child. Ellen Whitelaw had been the only person with whom he was able to communicate; as a result, the father had been asked by his wife to dismiss the girl. That Mr. Zeller is also estranged from his wife is noted in the fact that because of her coldness, he had made advances from time to time to the many maids who had worked for them.

The total alienation of the parents from their son is shown in a conversation that the three of them have about art, a vocation the Zellers airily dismiss as "useless" even though Bobby has decided to devote his life to it. We would have to range widely in modern fiction to find a scene equal in intensity and savageness to the one in which Bobby, defeated by his mother's inflexibility, finally shaves his beard—but not before he reviles both his parents for their loveless and selfish lives. At the end, all three of them sit in the same room simultaneously panting for freedom and release from one another.

In reading these tales of lovelessness and frustration between parents and children, we realize that Purdy needed only to look around the country to see how parents and their offspring live today to obtain the raw material for his tales. In witnessing the plight of many frustrated children, made so by parents who, for one reason or another, are unwilling themselves to grow mentally and are disinclined to allow their children to do so, Purdy would only be telling the truth about innumerable American families.

In any event, Purdy's talent to depict the inability of a mother and her adult son to establish a rapprochement is not a parochial but a universal one, as seen, for example, in "Eventide,"[7] in which the characters are all Negroes. Mahala's "smother" love has been the cause of her son Teeboy's running away from home and joining a dance band in which he plays tenor sax. She is unaware that everyone else knew that Teeboy was going to leave home. When Teeboy's band comes to town to play at the Music Box, Mahala cherishes the hope that she can lure her son back; and, for this purpose, she sends her younger sister Plumy on an exceedingly hot day to contact Teeboy. Enjoying his newly found freedom, he refuses to return. However, because of the nature of her visit and the great heat, Plumy has a vision of her own son, George Watson, who had died seventeen years earlier at the age of four. The poignancy of the tale lies in Mahala's reconciliation to Teeboy's loss only when it dawns on her that her sister is also a mother who has lost a son. Mahala had forgotten this fact in her selfish obsession to have Teeboy return. Equally moving is her realization that it is much easier to mourn for the loss of a son who has died at war—which she subconsciously wishes had been the case— than for one who has simply left home never to return. In blending the darkness of the night at the end of the story with Mahala's sense of loss, Purdy manages a perfect fusion of theme and atmosphere.

II *Where Husbands and Wives Differ*

The inability of parents to effect a rapport with their children may be viewed as one side or manifestation of the loveless condition in which these children were gestated; the other side is the inability or lack of desire on the part of one parent, or in some cases on the part of both, to grow and mature so as to surmount deficiencies or inanities of character. "Don't Call Me By My Right Name"[8] is probably one of the best examples of this shallow sense, for this story portrays the stupidity and even insanity of a woman's way of thinking about her newly married state. Middle-aged and only six months married to Frank Klein, with whom she had fallen in love even before she knew his last name, the recently espoused Lois Klein comes to the conclusion that her surname does not truly express her character. Thus at a social gathering where she begins to drink excessively, Lois begins pestering her husband to change his name. In the quarrel that follows, Frank, a long-suffering type whom the pressure of modern life has repeatedly beaten down, views this request as but another example of the many spiritual frustrations he has already endured. In a burst of rage he starts beating Lois.

Lois, finally rescued from Frank's fists, is questioned by some of the guests what she would change her name to; but she has no answer because she has not given this idea any previous thought. The whole confused tone of her reasoning is in perfect accord with the setting, for the gathering is "one of those fake dead long parties" where no one knew anyone else and where bodies could have been shoved through windows with no one being any the wiser until the following day. When Lois, bruised and drunk, finally joins her husband in the street where he fled after beating her, the kind of future in store for them is significantly foretold. Bleeding profusely from the mouth, where he had incessantly struck her, all Lois can call her husband, who is loath to call a taxi for her, is "son-of-a-bitch." This epithet she will no doubt often use in the future as she realizes she is stuck with Klein and his name. All told, the drunken atmosphere and the obtuseness of Lois's thought combines to highlight the nadir of a marriage where one of the members is concerned solely with changing her outer identity and with nothing more.

In "Man and Wife,"[9] it is more a psychic deviation in Lafe Kraus than it is shallow thinking that threatens his marriage to middle-aged Peaches Maud. At twenty-eight, Lafe has just been fired from his job for giving the impression of being a homosexual, which he in fact is. Giving special significance to Lafe's psychic woes is the fact that his mother had told Peaches Maud about her son's predilection for men during their engagement; nonetheless, Peaches Maud had decided to marry him. Now that he is fired, Peaches Maud is literally horrified at the impasse to which Lafe's deviant sexual behavior has brought their lives and marriage. Ironically, Lafe keeps asking her whether he has satisfied her sexually since they have been married, and he openly wonders whether or not he will be capable of doing so in the future. Even more dismaying to Peaches's already terrified sense of her situation is Lafe's promise that he will never leave her and that she will always be able to depend upon him, this to a woman who has never been able to hear "about anything that ain't human," thereby indicating her horror of homosexuality.

The entire conversation takes place in a room made unbearable by a hot July sun, and the dialogue is accompanied by the intermittent clatter of a refrigerator that is about to break down, as if to symbolize the emotional collapse of a mechanical marriage. Thus "Man and Wife" unerringly depicts the plight of two people who are locked together in a hellish marriage which from the beginning never had a chance at fulfillment. Maud's "Why did this have to happen to me" is appropriately matched by Lafe's realization that everything had come to an end just because of the way he eyed boys and men who, in turn, had decided that something was wrong with his character.

"Man and Wife" lacks the poignancy of "Sound of Talking,"[10] where we are introduced to the Farebrother couple, who, like Lafe and Peaches Maud, are also imprisoned in their own private hell. This time, however, the husband, Virgil Farebrother, is not a homosexual but a paraplegic victim of World War II; and he spends his waking hours in a wheelchair and endures severe pain in his crippled legs. To divert her husband's mind from his condition and to make herself believe that she does not mind living with him, Mrs. Farebrother has begun to lie occasionally. She concocts a fantastic tale in which a raven to which she had been attracted in a pet shop, kept repeating that someone had died. Virgil, who despises pets, is so taken in by the account as to offer to give her fifty dollars to purchase the bird since it might cheer her since he realizes the miserable company he has been because of his physical condition. But Mrs. Farebrother, for whom it is far more important that her husband want something for himself and not simply be preparing himself for death, rejects the offer.

Once more, in a mere seven pages, an unforgettable picture is limned. The two are tied together for life, and each of them is dying, the husband physically and the wife spiritually because of his condition. But until death's release, like the Kleins in "Don't Call Me By My Right Name," a cheerless future awaits the Farebrothers. For once the talk about the raven had been concluded early in the morning, another long day had begun which they of necessity would spend together. The story conveys a chilling sense of death-in-life as two people inexorably await their fate.

In two stories which reek of small-town life, "You Reach For Your Hat" and "A Good Woman," Purdy continues his unrelenting probe of the motives and the reasoning that wreak havoc with the lives of married people. Centering on the beautiful young widow Jennie Esmond, whose husband Lafe (not to be confused with Lafe in "Man and Wife") had died in World War I, the first tale[11] makes its special impact with the fact that Jennie does not engage in the mourning rites that her neighbors think she, as a widow should. To Mamie Jordan, one of Jennie's friends and an out-and-out sentimentalist, some of Jennie's actions seem almost heretical. She stays out late at the Mecca Saloon, a place that ladies—let alone widows—are not supposed to frequent; and, six months after learning that Lafe had been reported missing in action, Jennie has removed the gold star from her window. Mamie's views of life have been almost completely molded by Hollywood, with its emphasis on happy celluloid endings. Instead of missing Lafe, Jennie indicates that she had never really loved him: "I only pretended when we were together." Furthermore, she reveals that Lafe had in fact married her for merely physical reasons.

Yet in recounting to Mamie her empty life with Lafe before he had gone to war, Jennie, whose mother had ironically foretold a happy marriage for her beautiful daughter, begins to understand her late husband for the first time. Yet her illumination is short-lived, for there had been no real rapport from the start, and to Jennie it now seems that Lafe had never existed at all. Having heard these revelations of married life, Mamie is thunder-struck; and her ideal of connubial blass, as presented on the movie screen, is completely shattered. Jennie wishes she could say something fine about her relationship with Lafe so that she could leave Mamie with her "litle mental comforts," but she can find nothing solacing to say. For Jennie, there is nothing she can do about her sense of sorrow except wait for the houselights to go on and reach for her hat as if she were at a movie that had made her cry.

Only nine pages long, "You Reach for Your Hat" still offers an insightful commentary from a woman's point of view on the reasons for unsuccessful marriages. Jennie at least had been desirable sexually; but in "A Good Woman,"[12] the other tale

with a small-town setting, the reader is introduced to Maud,
a very plain young woman. Since her marriage to Obie, a former
orchestra leader turned traveling salesman, her life has revolved
around two activities: going to the movies with her friend
Mamie, and enjoying afterwards a strawberry ice-cream soda
at Mr. Hannah's drugstore. Mamie, an entirely different person
than the Mamie in "You Reach for Your Hat," had once lived
in St. Louis; but she is now reconciled to living in Martinsville.
Yet she is irked every now and then by the banalities of small-
town life, and she asks Maud what either of them is getting
out of life. A mental nonentity who would be content to spend
her life going to the movies and sipping sodas, Maud is disturbed by such questions, since they keep her from enjoying
her sodas. Maud's humdrum life is invaded by a crisis when she
is apprised by Mr. Hannah that she has a soda bill for thirty-five
dollars. Although he is obviously telling a lie, she cannot challenge him, for she has not kept a record of her own. Asked
to come to the back room where he will be able to explain the
bill in privacy, Maud is soon being hugged and kissed by the
old lecher, who keeps telling her that she is beautiful. Although
she succeeds in breaking away from his embraces, Maud, once
home, and still startled as a result of her ordeal, takes a look
at herself in the mirror. She fancies herself a beauty and she
believes she must have been one before Obie came along. In
her reminiscent mood, she recalls how years ago she and her
mother had walked along under her new parasol and joked
together, more like two young girls than mother and daughter.
From such flimsy recollections in a vacuous mind, and from
Maud's conversations with Mamie, the reader obtains the tone
and flavor of small-town life, which is on a par with the depictions of Sherwood Anderson and Edgar Lee Masters.

III   *Tales of Humor*

Not all of Purdy's talents are devoted to the creation of the
macabre and the grotesque in his portrayals of unhappy marriages and cruelty to children. In two minor narratives "You
May Safely Gaze" and 'Plan Now to Attend," he displays his
gifts as a humorist. In the former tale,[13] Guy, in the course of

a lunch hour, tells his friend Philip of his dislike of the recent shenanigans of two fellow workers, Milo and Milo's Austrian friend, both physical culture enthusiasts who work for the same firm as Guy. Giving special piquancy to Guy's complaint is the fact that the more he indicts his two coworkers and gives the reasons people should agree with him, the more he reveals how people who observe the two men exercising gain pleasure from watching their bulging muscles. Especially interested is the seventy-year-old boss of the three men involved, who happens to be a woman.

The climax occurs one day on a crowded beach when, before a huge throng that is literally mesmerized by the paces that the two muscle men are putting themselves through, both Milo and his friend simultaneously feel their swimming trunks split down the middle. Instead of feeling embarrassed, however, both men laugh uproariously at their mishap. Even Mae, Guy's wife, finds the situation amusing and tells her husband to mind his business if he finds the incident deplorable; as for herself, she wishes to be left to enjoy this unexpected spectacle. On the surface "You May Safely Gaze" is nothing more than a humorous indictment of the American passion for youthfulness; at the same time, we can't help sympathizing with Guy's remark that, after people pass thirty, they should be thinking of more important things than development of their bodies.

"Plan Now to Attend,"[14] on the other hand, is a more vigorous indictment of the smooth, bland, beneficial results that are supposed to follow the reading of such do-it-yourself religious best sellers as *The Power of Positive Thinking* and *Peace of Mind.* "Plan Now to Attend," set against a college reunion taking place in a large hotel, is chiefly concerned with the reactions of two classmates, Fred Parker and Ezra Graitop, who have not seen each other for twenty years. Remembering that Graitop had tried to convert him to atheism during their collegiate days, Fred learns that his classmate has since been converted and is now an important figure in the "new religion" movement. For Fred, the question becomes how Graitop could have advanced as far as he has. His lifeless expression at forty reminds Fred of a mannequin in a department store window and betrays the man's essential shallowness and alienation from life.

In the course of renewing their acquaintanceship, Graitop becomes so drunk that he needs to be taken to his room and put to bed; there Fred, looking at him intently, is amazed that, though they are both in their early forties, Ezra still looks like a sixteen-year-old boy; life and its trials have left him seemingly untouched. This contrasts with Fred's depleted condition, which is the result of heavy drinking every morning merely to get started at his job as a salesman. Even more disgusting to Fred is Graitop's evident lack of substance as a religionist. From his bed, he assures Fred that, although the latter is a typical sinner, he in time will see the light and that even now he is precious to Graitop's group. Such clichés and superficial utterances breed not only a hatred of religion but also a disregard for serious inquiries about the spiritual role it can play in one's life. Here in essence is a short but stinging indictment of religious phenomena and movements that promise man a better kind of life without stressing the tremendous efforts and regeneration that are necessary to obtain this objective.

IV   63: Dream Palace

A haunting novella in this first collection of stories, *63: Dream Palace* is one of the best, if not the best, piece of fiction that Purdy has so far written. In reviewing the narrative, William Bittner described its effect as the course the modern short story would have taken had not the tales of Hawthorne and Melville been circumvented by O'Henry and his surprise endings.[15] We can certainly agree with Bittner's statement, for the power of blackness and the consequent sense of tragedy, pity, and terror which the novella evokes are indeed pervasive. Told as a flashback, the novella is primarily concerned with the effect one Fenton Riddleway, a nineteen-year-old boy, has had on two older people—Parkhearst Cratty, a writer who somehow never got anything written; and Grainger, a beautiful, drunken forty-year-old heiress—both of whom had originally befriended Fenton, and who later were responsible for his death.

In the course of the opening conversation between these two, which leads to the flashback, Cratty and Grainger are revealed as literally lifeless lushes, who are unable to expunge the memory of Fenton from their lives. Hallucinated and surrealistic best describe the world they live in, and one in which the normal view of reality may well be a dream; still it is in this same eerie and frightening world that Fenton matures quickly because of the death of his mother and later of his brother Claire. On the other hand, Parkhearst and Grainger, lacking any real perception of life's values and relationships—and thus really "dead"— are left to regale each other about Fenton's sad fate.

What the flashback reveals is that Fenton, a handsome youth, and his younger, thirteen-year-old brother Claire, both recently orphaned, had left West Virginia to go to the big city, presumably Chicago or New York. There, alone on 63rd Street, they had waited in a badly dilapidated and deserted house, for Kincaid, a friend who had promised them a job. But, like the two protagonists in *Waiting for Godot*, they had waited in vain. Thus, with no one to look after them, with their supply of money beginning to run short, and with no skills or knowledge to obtain work of any kind, the boys had become frightened about their future prospects. When not in the house sharing with Claire the one cot available, Fenton spent his time either with the drifters in the city parks or at all-night-movie theaters in an effort to keep from thinking about his troubles. Well-meaning and desirous of doing the right thing, Fenton is the hillbilly lost in a large city. At this low point in his experience Cratty meets him in the park and befriends him.

If Fenton is mentally unsettled at this particular stage of his life, he is, even more, spiritually lost, a fact noted in his admission that he had desired his mother's death even before she died, and that he presently wishes Claire, who is ill, to die also. Yet he admits that his mother and brother are the only two people he has ever loved or even cared about. For Fenton, young as he is, life is already absurd as a result of his existential encounter with the world. In the little notes he keeps about his situation, he sees man as getting nowhere in this life. But, like the characters in *Waiting for Godot*, Fenton realizes that society expects one not to surrender, but to persist or simply to wait. That he was not at all content with this utterly pessimistic and hopeless state of affairs and that he found conventional religion of no help to him are seen in one thoughtful conversation Fenton has with Claire, the younger brother, who is confined to the house because of illness. Religiously inclined, Claire insists that he has heard God in the darkness of the house. Fenton scoffs at this idea, since he doubts God's existence. Later, in a conversation with Parkhearst at the latter's home, Fenton reveals that he would not be in the mess he is if God actually existed; he also wants to know whether his host believes in a supreme being. Parkheart's reply is that, while he does not believe there is a God, he is constantly mulling the matter over in his mind.

We feel that Fenton, who desperately wants to believe and to forgo his nihilistic course, would have had something substantial to think about had Cratty's reply been an affirmative one. But how could Cratty have had any real concept of a supreme being when his own life has been spiritually null and void? Twenty-nine-years-old and married, Cratty is a kept man who, when not with Grainger—whose hired companion he is—spends his time studying people in the park, ostensibly to write stories about them, which never get written. In fact, the wildness and freedom which he sees in Fenton's eyes when they first meet make Cratty realize how much of his own manhood he has lost, and in a wild rage he determines to turn the boy over to Grainger to ruin. For this task Grainger is eminently qualified, for, like Cratty, she also lives in a spiritual vacuum. This last fact is seen in her concept of happiness, which envisions life as a beautiful garden filled with people that she enjoys, with drinking the eternal activity. A decade earlier she had lost her husband Russell and is now in need of another companion to keep her company in the ten-year-long spree she has been on. This was the unenviable position Fenton was meant to fill, and with a woman who is held in such low regard that the only thing Cratty's drinking companions admire her for is the excellent drinking parties she is constantly giving. It is no wonder then that she drinks incessantly, probably hoping this activity will fill the void both in her life and in her dream palace, haunted as they both are by a sense of purposelessness and death.

The portrait of this aging lush is reminiscent of those actresses in Hollywood films who, either because of the advent of the talkies or the loss of their acting ability, hole themselves up in their grand Beverly Hills mansions or on Sunset Boulevard to spend the rest of their lives in drink and lust. Grainger is one of Purdy's finest portraits, one in which he depicts the power of ruined but wealthy people to wreak havoc with the lives of others.

When Fenton is introduced to Grainger's mansion and its corruption, nothing matters to him anymore. In one sense, Fenton's plight is similar to Salinger's Holden Caulfield, whose contacts with adults revealed nearly all of them to be "phony" or corrupt. But, where Holden found some solace in the innocence of childhood as exemplified by his sister Phoebe, Fenton finds the universe to be meaningless. He wants to believe, he wants to be reborn, but he sees nothing in this life designed for that purpose. This being so, his decision to throw in his lot with Grainger, to marry her if need be, brings about the horrifying climax.

Realizing that Claire, with his better sense of values, would hinder him in his endeavor to lead the glittering *vita nuova* that both Cratty and Grainger had in store for him, Fenton kills his younger brother. In this act there is also a perverse sense of love that would remove the boy from a hateful world. And in the heartrending scene in which he carries his brother's body up to the attic and places it in a chest, Fenton utters the phrase "up we go then, motherfucker," which in context seems sacrilegious, but which Dame Edith Sitwell has so validly interpreted as Fenton's understanding of the dead boy's desire to return to his mother, whom he had loved.[16]

Permeating the novella, like a voice crying in the wilderness, is Fenton's quest for identity—for an answer to the riddle of the universe. Thus in the scene in which Fenton becomes involved with a group of homosexuals and actors at a party, he is plainly told by one of the guests that no one is responsible for him or for his actions, thereby reminding the reader of a similar situation in Stephen Crane's "The Open Boat." Using a choice four-letter word, Fenton then inquires who might be responsible for him. In a world in which God does not exist and where there is no viable substitute, the universe becomes similar to the one conceived by Ivan Karamazov in which everything is permitted; therefore, Fenton's murder of Claire seems justified, since it removes the one obstacle which prevents his enjoyment of Grainger's tremendous wealth.

Horrifying as the climax is and similar to a Greek tragedy in the overwhelming effect and catharsis which it evokes, 63: Dream Palace also has a tremendous impact in that it provokes sympathy and pity for troubled "loners" like Fenton Riddleway. They ask the right questions; but, for one reason or another, they fail to receive legitimate answers. Making Fenton's situation even more tragic is that, in selling out to people like Grainger and Cratty, he surrenders himself to those who are in a position to corrupt beyond redemption his fundamentally innocent character. In a questionnaire that inquired of contemporary writers which of their works they were ready to reread at this point in their careers, Purdy chose 63: Dream Palace, and he did so with good reason.[17] For this novella, together with a few other pieces Purdy has written, are easily the best of their kind in our day. James Michie has aptly observed that "Purdy's best stories are extraordinarily powerful, lit by a hard light, and observed as if through the unblinking eye of a tiger or a child.... He deals with archetypal passions: they strike his characters with the sudden force of a natural disaster to produce the inexplicable acts which the ancients attributed to possession by a god but for which nowadays Man must somehow bear the responsibility."[18]

CHAPTER 3

Novels of Fantasy and Realism: Malcolm *and* The Nephew

P URDY'S ability to write macabre and grotesque tales of a high order was convincingly demonstrated in *Color of Darkness*, and the next natural step for him would have been to try his hand at fashioning a full-length novel; this step he took in *Malcolm*, which was published in 1959. In the novel form, a writer can really elaborate upon his vision of life, which, if powerful enough, can gain him a surer literary immortality than that afforded by his shorter works. We have only to think about Hawthorne's tales or the novellas of Henry James, as compared with *The Scarlet Letter* and *The Portrait of a Lady*, to realize that the greater impact of these two longer works lies in the fuller treatments of the themes. In *The Scarlet Letter*, Hawthorne was able to explore deeply the Puritan ethos; in *The Portrait of a Lady*, James was afforded an opportunity for his complex presentation of European decadence versus American innocence.

I   *Maturing Insights into American Life*

In a similar sense Purdy's first novel *Malcolm* furnished him with the opportunity to portray on a larger scale than in his short fiction his developing discernments of modern American life and society. However, where *Color of Darkness* had received more or less laudatory acclaim, *Malcolm* was the recipient of mixed reviews. To be sure, there were critics like Donald Cook who found the novel to be one of "marvelous freshness,"[1] while David Daiches was won over by the opening sentence with its combination of the "beautiful matter-of-fact clarity of a fairy tale, the stark realism of the documentary, and the provocative

43

deadpan of the satire."[2] On the other hand, while lauding Purdy's disciplined style, Granville Hicks frankly admitted he was not at all sure what Purdy's intent was in his first novel.[3] Again, there were those reviewers who, tired of Purdy's treatment of the grotesque, openly wondered when the novelist would ever come to grips with the familiar and everyday aspects of life.[4] Still another critic admitted that it was far easier to tell what *Malcolm* was *about* than what it actually *was*.[5]

Had the last-mentioned reviewer taken the time to ponder seriously the book's underlying theme, he would have realized that the novel was essentially an allegory in which an innocent, easygoing, friendly, and very handsome fifteen-year-old youngster is introduced to "mod" America and experience. Too, the reviewers might have noted that *Malcolm* belongs to that line of American novels running from Mark Twain's *Huckleberry Finn* through Hemingway's *A Farewell to Arms* to Salinger's *The Catcher in the Rye*—a type which sets the innocent in an indifferent or hostile world that he cannot understand. And the bizarre people Malcolm meets and the zany adventures that he undergoes combine to tell an almost Kafkaesque tale— Kafkaesque in the sense that although Malcolm is exposed to such aspects of contemporary American life as marriage, sex, science, art, and wealth, these exposures lead to nothing illuminating or constructive, but instead to the boy's spiritual as well as physical death. The novel is, in fact, a parody of the Romance form: in the Romance the hero usually emerges as the victor at the end of his quest, but just the reverse occurs in Malcolm's case.

Structured as a picaresque tale so as to accentuate Malcolm's homelessness in a world of strangers, *Malcolm* was subtitled "a comic novel," thereby indicating Purdy's primary intent. It certainly is humorous as one funny episode or gesture or remark follows another, but this hilarity is always accompanied by the progressive death of Malcolm's innocence in the midst of corruption. Set against the background of the bland, prosperous Eisenhower years, with "normalcy" and laissez-faire the tenor of the times, the novel can be viewed symbolically as the death-in-life of modern American society, which Purdy views as well on its way to self-destruction; and the reason lies in the false and empty values which had developed during the 1950s because of unbridled individualism and rank materialism.

Among the various people Malcolm encounters in his pilgrimage, not a single one has anything of an affirmative or a constructive nature to offer him in his search for knowledge and experience. In fact, the very first person Malcolm meets is one Estel Blanc, a retired black undertaker who bids Malcolm to return some twenty years later when he has grown up. Might not Blanc's request signify that, as Malcolm matures and becomes aware of the corruption around him, he will see the death of the human spirit around him? Having observed this death, Malcolm will then truly be ready for a meeting with the undertaker. Thus, we may draw the inference that an introduction to death is the first step in getting to know anything about life in America.

II   *Modern Marriages—U.S.A. Style*

Malcolm's journey takes him to the homes of three married couples, the Raphaelsons, the Girards, and the Braces. These people know one another because of their common interest in art—either as painters or as collectors. Sending Malcolm to these people is Mr. Cox, an astrologer-pederast. Seeing the lad, who has apparently been abandoned by his father, sitting daily on a bench outside a most palatial hotel, Cox decides to introduce the boy to life. Cox is in fact a latter-day Mephistopheles who sets the youngster on his Faustian quest, and Malcolm is certainly a Lockean cipher who needs to be filled in by experience.

More importantly, Cox serves as the mouthpiece of a decaying American culture when he advises Malcolm to yield himself completely to experience in his quest; therefore, he underlines from the outset the extreme materialism which will envelop the boy.[6] Furthermore, Cox strives to bring forth certain predetermined results by having what he considers to be the right people come together to produce these results; in fact, he is much like certain television programs that bring young men and women together as a result of a computer's output. Cox thus appears to be a representative of the faith that too many moderns have come to place in the power of science and its precise phenomena to straighten out irrational human affairs. That Cox is known as a pederast by most of the people to whom he sends Malcolm is indicative of the sexually aberrant condition in which the boy's quest will be pursued from the beginning. Cox's homosexuality understood, it would seem natural in context that the three married couples to whom he sends Malcolm have marriages that are also in parlous and desperate states because of sexual delinquencies and infidelities. Since Malcolm spends a good part of his time with one or another of these couples, he is introduced to a devastating view of modern matrimony. For, in the lives of these different couples, we observe the same recurring and depressing pattern of loveless and barren unions that Purdy had previously delineated in many of the stories in *Color of Darkness*. This time, however, the emptiness of the couples' lives is accentuated by the abundant swilling of liquor by nearly everyone involved.

When Malcolm comes along with his charming sense of innocence, the married couples view him as the one factor that would make their lives less empty. Attempts to "adopt" him by each of the couples fail because they regard him primarily as a possession and not as a person, thus revealing their distorted values. The Raphaelsons, whom Malcolm meets first, are divided by the highly divergent goals that they pursue. Kermit Raphaelson, a midget, is an artist whose paintings no one wants to buy. Laureen, his Amazon wife and an ex-whore, had expected marriage to straighten her out sexually; now, however, she seeks a divorce. Here, in the union of a midget and a veritable Amazon and their marital hang-ups, we have a fine example of Purdy's grotesque and fantastic imagination at its very best.

Bizarre yet understandable is Laureen's desire for a divorce, based as it is on her refusal to acquiesce to her husband's request to have her once again ply her old trade. For Kermit is not really interested in becoming a successful painter as much as he is in living a luxurious life, and he believes his wife's extramarital activities would make that possible. No son of Raphael is this Raphaelson; he is a midget both in perception and size. Disappointed in Laureen's refusal to go along with his plan, he suffers an even greater blow to his self-esteem when she runs off with a Japanese wrestler, whose sexual equipment, we are told, is superior to his. Nor is this episode the end of Laureen's adventures in wedlock. The hallucinated sense of reality in the lives of these two characters is characteristic of the lives of practically all the characters Malcolm encounters. And one reason that Purdy's underlying savage satires of wedlock and other aspects of American life are often missed by the casual reader may be that the many zany and hilarious episodes tend to elicit guffaws instead of reflection.

Carrying on the hoax of modern marriage are the enormously wealthy Girards, the second couple that Malcolm befriends.[7] Their great wealth, however, has been of little avail in making a twenty-year-old marriage a union of the heart; for Madame Girard (as she likes to be addressed) is, like Laureen Raphaelson, intent on leaving her husband; but why the Girards should have ever married in the first place is difficult to understand. An imperious dipsomaniac who always needs to feel victorious over everyone else in every situation, Madame Girard, far from viewing matrimony as a tender trap, regards it instead as a snare which snaps shut on everything she holds dear. On the other hand, her husband, who had worshipped his wife as a goddess from the outset of their marriage, has since grown tired of her haughty and imperious manner. As a result, he has managed to satisfy himself with a host of other women who have ranged from laundry women to grande dames. Learning of these escapades, Madame Girard at last intends to divorce him. Much to her consternation, however, she is doffed by her husband when he meets Laureen Raphaelson, who has tired of her Oriental lover and is now ready to marry Girard, who wants to have the heirs that his first wife has failed to give him.

Just as joyless and sordid as the Raphaelson and the Girard marriages is the relationship between Jerome and Eloisa Brace, the third couple Malcolm meets.[8] Eloisa Brace, a hard-drinking blonde, left a rich husband for Jerome, who, she tells Malcolm, does not give her a day off, sexually speaking. Yet she prefers Jerome, since her previous spouse did not desire her often enough. That she cannot help but go on consorting with the many black jazz musicians who frequent her house is yet another matter, but one Jerome knew about when he married her. Jerome Brace is an ex-convict who cannot find work and whose inability to adjust to the life outside the penitentiary is reflected in a book he has written and has humorously entitled *They Could Have Me Back.* Another example of Purdy's humor is that while he has Brace working on a study of juvenile delinquency, he has him simultaneously contribute to this type of behaviour by having him make sexual advances toward Malcolm.

Eloisa, like Kermit Raphaelson, is a painter who is more interested in the money to be obtained from painting than in producing a work of art. Since Madame Girard will pay ten thousand dollars for a portrait of Malcolm which Eloisa has painted and for which she has only wanted five thousand, the world of art in *Malcolm* is dictated more by the profit motive of its painters than by their desire to produce works of solid worth. Moreover, the art collectors are concerned only with prestige.

Absurd, disordered, and lacking in values as the lives of these couples might seem to some, pathos is the only feeling their actions stimulate. They represent types who live and have their nonbeing in the various bohemian or Gold Coast areas of our country. Nothing about these people is truly constructive and vital, and they merely serve as Malcolm's mentors on marriage; but all he learns from them is that marriage is a farce. However, the most trenchant and the most damning example of the burlesque that matrimony has supposedly become in our time is Malcolm's own ill-fated union with Melba, a chanteuse and a nymphomaniac. Although only a couple of years older than he, she is already twice a divorcée. She is the one person Malcolm manages to meet without the help of Mr. Cox, who has informed him that anyone who really matters is already married. And though Malcolm is thoroughly conditioned to find wedlock naturally joyless and sordid, thanks to the three couples, the boy's acceptance of Cox's view makes him a ready initiate to the institution.

That Malcolm might have waited until he was more mature for this important step is ruled out by a tongue-in-cheek author: Malcolm has two drawbacks—he is too young for the service and is also insufficiently schooled to obtain a decent job. What, then, is there for him to do but get married?[9] Looking at a good many American mothers and the pressures they put on their daughters to get married whether or not they are so inclined, we realize how true Purdy's indictment is. This view of wedlock— that all must enter into it at one time or another—is developed later in *Cabot Wright Begins*, where the desire to remain single is thought of as abhorrent.

Melba has Malcolm, hitherto a virgin, hustled off to a whore-house to learn what will be expected of him in his nuptial bed. En route to the brothel, he visits a tattoo establishment where he is branded like an animal. These episodes symbolize the bestial nature of his future sexual activities with Melba the nymphomaniac, and the boy's death shortly thereafter from excessive drinking and Melba's incessant sexual demands is anti-climactic. Malcolm's fate is in keeping with everything he has learned about married life, and his death is a fitting conclusion to his quest for knowledge.

Wildly and grotesquely ludicrous as some of the incidents and episodes are, we feel only a sense of revulsion to this kind of Black Humor; for a vast cancer in the form of animality seems to be eating away at the vitals of society. This impression is intensified by an almost total lack of the affection and devotion that marriage partners are normally expected to share. Significant, too, in the four marriages discussed, is the fact that very little mention is ever made of children—as if the author intends to indicate that the barrenness of feeling in which each union was conceived leads only to sterility and futility.

III   *The Weaknesses of* Malcolm

The major weakness of the novel lies in the character of Malcolm himself: the fact that he, whose innocence and friendli-ness win almost immediately all the people he visits, is never once seen gaining any real insight into life from his experiences, similar to that gained by two earlier questers, Somerset Maugham's Philip Carey and James Joyce's Stephen Dedalus. In their search for manhood and self-knowledge, they occasion-ally gain clear glimpses—Carey, with his realization that life's pattern is very much that of a variegated rug; Dedalus, with his perception that only in the smithy of his soul could he forge the conscience of his race. But no insight of this kind is ever permitted Malcolm.

Like Fenton Riddleway, Malcolm walks the road to corruption
without blinking an eye; but where Fenton, in seeking truth,
finds nothing but a God who is dead to all human needs and
affairs, Malcolm never has any such complicated spiritual dilem-
mas or such opportunities for religious rejection. Waiting to
have experience imprinted upon him, he is merely used by all
with whom he comes in contact—and always for selfish reasons.
Really a mental cipher, Malcolm views life as a shiny, chrome-
like affair; and its dazzle hides the depravity which lurks
everywhere. In his journey towards knowledge, Malcolm brings
to mind such contemporary seekers as J. D. Salinger's Holden
Caulfield, Joseph Heller's Yossarian, and Ralph Ellison's nameless
hero in *Invisible Man*. Where Holden would keep children from
falling over the cliff by serving as the catcher in the rye; and
where Yossarian would flee from certain death by his realization
that in order to stay alive in an essentially insane world one
must flee from it; and where Ellison's young man for a short
time views Communism as the solution to society's ills—Malcolm
has no similar ideas to animate him. He is, in fact, more acted
upon than acting; for the Raphaelsons, the Girards, and the
Braces all try to manipulate him for their respective selfish ends.

Concomitant to Malcolm's failure to grow mentally is his
tendency to feel sleepy at the very moment so-called crises occur
in the lives of those he has come to know. All that this drowsy
feeling might denote to a mind that is open, as Malcolm's is,
almost solely to sensory impressions, is that sleep is just as
important an action as any other, or that sleep, in the sense of
vacuity, is the only reaction that the activities of the married
couples produce in him. Thus, when Laureen is inveighing
against Kermit and threatening to divorce him, the boy falls
asleep. Had he waited just a few moments longer, he would
have seen them engage in copulation after their quarreling had
ceased. Again, in the scene where Madame Girard is threatening
to divorce her husband, Malcolm's drowsy handsomeness completely fascinates her; she stops her tirade and pesters her
husband to have the boy come to live with them and be their love.

There are moments, of course, when Malcolm and some others
make efforts to break through the hallucinatory proceedings in
which they are engaged and when they seek something more

meaningful in their experience. For example, when told by
Jerome Brace that what he and Malcolm believe in is far superior
to anything entertained by Girard and Mr. Cox, Malcolm, interestingly enough, is never told what this belief is.[10] Again, when
Girard pleads desperately with the boy to live with him and
his new spouse Laureen, claiming he is desperately alone, even
though married, the magnate leaves and never returns to learn
Malcolm's response. Earlier, when Malcolm is confronted with
the query as to whether he has come to visit Kermit and
Laureen simply for themselves or solely at Cox's behest, we
are shown how hungry Laureen is for simple recognition as
a person.

All told, however, these attempts to arrive at some meaningful sense of reality are doomed. Symbolic of this futility is the
highly polished passage, characteristic of Purdy's descriptive
style at its best, of the lovely interior of Eloisa's house with its
various *objets d'art*. Here the time seems to be always late
afternoon, and the atmosphere is languorous and reminiscent
of Tennyson's *The Lotos Eaters*. But all this loveliness is destined
to shrivel and become dust, we are told, simply because something is wrong with the mechanism of the universe.[11] Probably
the best expression of this sense of futility is voiced by George
Leeds, one of the Negro musicians who frequents Eloisa's house.
The point, he tells Malcolm, is to live one's life so as not to
become involved in the affairs of others.[12] This desire to stay
disengaged from any meaningful encounter with others is perhaps
best evidenced by Melba, who, while conscious that her nymphomania is causing her husband's death, keeps downing pills
that obliterate all sense of grief and guilt. Thus does conscience
make cowards of us all.

Malcolm is additionally weakened by the ambiguity Purdy
employs at the very end. The search for his father, for example,
which had been one of the goals of Malcolm's quest, is negated
when, before his death, he questions whether in fact his father
ever existed. Again, to have the boy die and then to have Madame Girard intimate that neither his corpse nor any other corpse
was interred at his funeral are to make the sense of the grotesque
pervading the novel appear absolutely inane. We wonder why
this burial scene was included, except perhaps to suggest that

the lives of those associated with Malcolm were of such stuff as dreams are made of. Malcolm's innocence and friendliness may in a sense have appeared as a dream to these people whose sense of reality resided in more earthy matters.

These deficiencies aside, the fact remains that, unlike an earlier fictional hero Candide, who learned from experience to remain alive and later to tend his garden, *Malcolm* makes clear that no such satisfactory ending is possible in our society in our day; for innocence and friendliness in children seemingly exist for no other purpose than to be corrupted and destroyed by adults who themselves are mere children in perception.

IV *The Strengths of* Malcolm

The strong points of the novel derive from the weaknesses just discussed. By portraying the four futile marriages as he does, Purdy is apparently asking his fellow Americans to consider more seriously the shambles that many of them have made of their lives, particularly of their marriages. While many of the episodes depicting these couples are funny, to say the least, this fun becomes for the serious reader the basis for the consideration of the following questions: What makes a marriage successful in the long run; and how can one equip himself to be successful in this respect? With the divorce rate ever mounting all over the world, let alone in our country, we begin to understand the enormity of the problem and what it might mean to the future as far as stable family life is concerned.

Aside from what makes marriage a success, there is the related problem of people getting married, as Malcolm did, simply because there was nothing else at that time for which he was prepared. At a period when maturity is so desperately needed, there seems to be altogether too much emphasis on wedlock for the mere sake of wedlock. Purdy seems to be indicating that many people are much too shallow for marriage and that they should first grow mentally before taking this important step. Again, single people who are self-sufficient and find themselves good company belie the fact that marriage is a be-all and end-all of life.

Finally, we have the scene in which something in the mechanism of the universe is blamed for the dissolution of the beautiful, timeless autumnal tone that holds forth in the interior of Eloisa's house. At this point, we actually wonder whether it is the mechanism that is at fault. It would seem rather that the characters, in having committed themselves to nothing higher than their respective self-indulgences and selfish ways, are consigned to a futile and essentially sterile existence. In this instance, Purdy seems to be questioning the values of his fellow Americans and to be demanding a higher dedication to something other than things, even though these may be priceless *objets d'art*. All told, *Malcolm*, though a "comic novel," leaves us pondering about the spiritual and mental bankruptcy characteristic of much of contemporary American life. Therein lies the chief strength of the novel.

V The Nephew—*A Realistic Novel of the Midwest*

For whatever reason—whether Purdy's appetite for the grotesque and the fantastic had temporarily been sated with *Malcolm*, or whether he had been nettled by the criticism that he was unable to or simply could not portray realistically the familiar aspects of everyday life—Purdy completely forsook in *The Nephew* the bizarre, cosmopolitan world he had fashioned in *Malcolm*. In its stead he created a world that had its roots in the conventional small-town life of the Middlewest where he had grown up. Utterly rejecting any attempt to shock, as he had done in *Malcolm*, Purdy wrote a low-keyed narrative of nothing more exciting than the efforts of a spinster aunt, Alma Mason, to obtain material for writing a memorial to Cliff, her nineteen-year-old nephew of the title, who had been killed in the Korean War.

This war sets the time of the novel's action which begins on one Memorial Day and ends exactly a year later. *The Nephew*, an excellently crafted novel, is a solid contribution to Realistic, modern fiction. Yet we can understand Richard Foster's comment that the book is "lifeless and depthless,"[13] for it explores rather cursorily the lives of almost a dozen quite unremarkable people. But in Alma's quest to obtain knowledge about Cliff from these people, she becomes a far more understanding person by the end of the narrative than the prim, retired elementary school-teacher she is at its outset. Alma learns a startling number of things about herself, about her townspeople, and, most of all, about her nephew, whom she feels she did not get to know as well as she should have in the four years he lived with her before he enlisted. So acutely and interestingly are these revelations presented in the narrative that they merit the tribute from William Peden, who wrote that if a more impressive novel had appeared in 1960, he had not heard about it.[14]

Time should confirm Peden's judgment; for, all told, *The Nephew* is the wisest, most compassionate novel that Purdy has so far written, and in it his portrayal of human weaknesses and frailties is distinctively softened. To be sure, the author's satiric bent is still operative, but the prevailing tone is one of gentleness, except when certain human idiocies evoke his ridicule. But nowhere in the novel do we find the unmitigated satire that characterized the work of an earlier Midwesterner Sinclair Lewis and his exposé of the same geographical terrain. Instead, Purdy's portrait of the quirks of character and the frustrations that beset people in their daily rounds make *The Nephew* more like an up-to-date version of Sherwood Anderson's *Winesburg, Ohio*. And, as in Anderson's classic, the regionalism and the touches of local color—such as the ketchup plant with its odor of boiling tomatoes that assails the nostrils of the townspeople each summer—make *The Nephew* a representative novel of middle America in our day.

VI *The World of Rainbow Center*

The action of *The Nephew* takes place in a town ironically named Rainbow Center where Alma Mason and her widower brother Boyd, an octogenarian real estate broker, live together. The kind of persons whose faces and characters could very well have served as models of Grant Wood's famous *American Gothic*, the Masons and their home serve as the focal point from which Alma seeks from her friends and neighbors a better appreciation of her deceased relative. Having spent most of her adult life teaching out of the state, Alma has not known her neighbors as well as she thought. Indeed, she begins to discover for the first time the private hells and purgatories in which most of them live; she learns as well the differing interpretations or concepts of her nephew that each of them entertains.

Probing below the seemingly placid surface, the reader once again uncovers such typical Purdian themes as loveless marriages, thoughtless and cruel parents, unloved children, and persons with small-town prejudices. These crosses many of Alma's neighbors bear. In fact, only one of Alma's friends, Clara Himbaugh, the Christian Science practitioner who acts with more zeal than wisdom in seeking proselytes among her Methodist neighbors, appears to be without a sense of joylessness and depression. However, in presuming to know the way of religious salvation much better than the people around her, Clara, for not acting more wisely and lovingly in her relationship to herself as well as to others, deserves the rather critical portrait drawn of her.[15]

Clara Himbaugh is only one of Alma's neighbors, all of whom form a microcosm in which their actions mirror those of the larger world outside Rainbow Center. The most unforgettable neighbor is probably Mrs. Barrington, the "old monarch" as she is affectionately known to the townspeople. A nonagenarian who has a limb injury that should have hampered her movements much of her adult life, Mrs. Barrington has managed to live an almost completely independent life devoted to such activities as community affairs, trips to Washington, and, most of all, gardening. Deeply appreciative of nature and its beauties, she manages to share this love with others with the trumpet vine she has been growing over one end of her property; for, when it blooms, it is beautiful enough to draw people from all over the state. Envied by her neighbors, who believe that she has enjoyed and derived more from life than they have, the "old monarch" has her own private woe: the realization that her deceased husband had never really loved her. She reveals this belief to Alma, who has always thought otherwise. Mrs. Barrington's rejection, however, has given her the needed insight for understanding Alma's problem—to determine whether or not Cliff had really learned to care for and love his aunt and uncle before he enlisted. She reassures Alma that her own experience has taught her that all that counts is one's own expression of love, regardless of whether it is accepted or rejected.[16]

Unlike Mrs. Barrington, Willard Baker, the Masons' next-door neighbor, has led a life of total waste; for he has devoted himself almost exclusively to excessive drinking and to all-night parties. Willard's carousings disgust Boyd Mason, a temperate person, who is disturbed equally by his neighbor's profligacy and by the noise that keeps him awake at night. Living with Willard in a homosexual relationship is his young companion, Vernon Miller. When we search for a reason for this relationship, we find that the misguided actions of Willard's dead mother had affected the life of her son: Mrs. Baker's constant and open preference for her younger son Joe rather than for Willard had made the older boy feel spiritless and unwanted. Ironically enough, Mrs. Baker's favoritism causes Joe, who later practices medicine with his father, to disgrace his family by his affair with a married woman and, ultimately, to commit suicide. Also ironic is Boyd's inability to comprehend to any great degree the course that Willard's life has taken in adulthood; for, of all the people privy to the way Mrs. Baker treated her two boys, Boyd knew best the sense of estrangement that Willard had suffered as a child.[17]

The pitiable person Willard has become through the years as he lives in the house left him by his parents is poignantly indicated when young Vernon determines to leave Rainbow Center. Terrified at the thought of facing the future alone, Willard bribes the young man to stay by promising to leave him his entire estate when he himself dies. Willard does so, and he dies almost immediately afterwards in an automobile accident. Having inherited a fair sum of money and eager to rid himself of the past, Vernon decides to marry Faye Laird, one of the few persons with whom Alma has a good relationship.

A French instructor for more than twenty years at the state college located in the town, Faye, like Alma, seems destined for a life of spinsterhood before Vernon enters her life. She visits Alma—one "old maid" asks advice from another on the subject of marriage. This scene would be comic were it not for the tragedy that has been for years the essence of Faye's life. Her mother had forced Faye years ago to give up a most eligible young man with whom she was in love. As a result, most of Faye's adult experience outside the classroom has been spent in supporting and caring for her mother, who has grown increasingly demented.

In Mrs. Laird's rare lucid moments, she is, however, the source of some of the funniest passages in the book, as she comments about every conceivable subject that she has learned about from watching television. Whether she is watching cowboys gunning down Indians or Old Glory on the television screen, her interpretations, derived as they are from a conservative area of the country, are characteristically those espoused by the political right wing and are the only light moments in a work that is otherwise sober, and at times grim.

VII *The Tawdry Lives of College Professors*

Aside from the pretensions of Clara Himbaugh, the Christian Science practitioner, the other object of Purdy's deep aversion is the administration of the state college, which is severely taken to task for its profession of lofty principles while simultaneously treating teachers like pawns in matters of promotion and dismissal. This indictment, which is made by Faye Laird in a letter of resignation that she writes in order to marry Vernon, focuses upon the shabby treatment afforded Professor Mannheim, a history teacher who had been Cliff's instructor before the boy had gone to war. That Mannheim has not become a full professor in the many years he has taught at the college has not been due to his inability either as a teacher or as a scholar; nor has it resulted from either his having been an avowed Marxist when he first arrived in Rainbow Center or from his early penchant for seducing coeds who became infatuated with him. As the college president views Mannheim's status, his fault has been his failure to give speeches before the Kiwanis and Rotary groups; moreover, Mannheim's frequent absences from banquets given at the end of the football season have not endeared him to the administration. Mannheim, now sixty, and requiring the aid of a cane for his walks, is merely ticking away the days before he can retire at sixty-five with a small pension.

A more graphic description of the torments besetting an impecunious middle-aged professor would be difficult to find in modern fiction. Mannheim, morbidly fearful of losing his posi-

tion before he retires, becomes almost hysterical with fear when
he is unexpectedly summoned to Mrs. Barrington's home. The
reason for his fear, we learn, is that years ago, as a member
of the Board of Trustees, the "old monarch" had plumped for his
dismissal on charges of moral turpitude. Now summoned solely
to give his reminiscences about Cliff as material for Alma's
memorial, but unaware of this innocent objective, the man becomes literally petrified because he thinks the invitation is a
ruse to oust him from his teaching post.

Mannheim's second wife Rosa also has an insecure life. Once
a coed from town, she had let him make love to her while his
first wife was dying. Feeling a sense of guilt that he could love
two women simultaneously, and while one of them was dying,
Mannheim had been compelled to reveal his situation to Cliff,
who had proved sensitive enough to listen to his professor's
affaires de coeur; otherwise, as we learn, Mannheim would have
committed suicide because of his pent-up emotions.

At this stage in their lives, Rosa Mannheim is completely dis-
enchanted with the man she had once respected; and she has
become the epitome of everything drab and cautious in her
desire to share eventually the pitiful income that her husband's
pension will bring. That her marriage has been a typically
Purdian one is emphasized by the poignant scene in which
Mannheim returns home from Mrs. Barrington's to inform her
of the reason he had been summoned to the old monarch's home.
His recital over, he asks to be left alone to finish writing an
article—a rejection that she has endured many times in the past
and one to which she can only grudgingly acquiesce with a
sense of despair.[18]

Rounding out the cluster of characters whom Alma gets to
know better in behalf of Cliff's memorial is the brainless Mrs.
Van Tassel, originally a friend of Alma's mother. An intellectual
nonentity, Mrs. Van Tassel is yet charitable enough to allow
her home to become the residence of the widowed Minnie Clyde
Hawke, an inveterate alcoholic who keeps a flask hidden in
her cane. Hilarious as the moment is when Mrs. Van Tassel
comes upon her boarder with her cane open, brandy flask out,
and its contents being swilled, Mrs. Hawke, next to Willard
Baker, is perhaps the most pitiable figure in the novel. She is

unsuccessful in her attempt to cure her addiction to liquor, and even her attempt at suicide fails.

VIII   *A More Understanding Alma*

Alma learns much in the period between the two Memorial Days, and from the unlikeliest sources. She even sees that those upon whom society frowns for their immoral or antisocial practices have something constructive to offer. In addition to having made himself the thoughtful receptacle of Mannheim's confession of adultery, Cliff, Alma discovers, had been deeply loved by Vernon Miller, simply because he had treated the man as a human being and not as a homosexual who had to be tolerated. In fact, so deeply had Vernon cared for Cliff's understanding of his situation, that he turned over to the youth a gift of four thousand dollars, originally given to Miller by Mrs. Barrington were he to leave Willard Baker and Rainbow Center for good. Vernon wanted Cliff to use the money to get away from the restrictions of small-town life and to start a new life elsewhere.

Among the changes we witness in Alma is her attitude to Mrs. Hawkes. Alma, who always entertained a great contempt for this excessive drinker, begins to view her in a totally different light when she learns that this woman's financial gift, with absolutely no strings attached, has helped Mrs. Van Tassel retain possession of her home. Moreover, by the time of Faye Laird's hour of need for moral support in her decision to marry Vernon Miller, Alma has become flexible enough to encourage her younger friend to act in accord with her intuition. At the beginning of the novel, Alma could not have given such advice; she had to first gain new insight and wisdom, and she did so as she learned more about her various neighbors.

Even Boyd Mason, who is at loggerheads on most matters with his old maid sister, begins to sense the truth that Cliff had cared for him and Alma, although the boy had never expressed his feeling to them. The scene at the end in which Alma and Boyd sit together in the dark nurturing the truth that, although they had never really gotten to know the nephew they had loved, he too had loved them—and their discernment creates an almost reverential tone. Interesting also at this point is Alma's recognition that she will never write the memorial as she had previously intended. This nonperformance reminds us of Parkhearst Cratty, who also never wrote any stories, although he was by vocation a writer. Another comparison exists, for, just as Cratty and Grainger talk about Fenton Riddleway only after he is dead, so do Alma and Boyd express their feelings about Cliff only after he has left them.

A complete turnabout from the world of *Malcolm*, and written in the deadpan manner that is reminiscent of some of Twain's works of the 1880s, *The Nephew* may be read by more people than some of Purdy's other works simply because of the quieter and more somber tone in which its human concerns are presented. Moreover, Purdy proves that, in writing about dull people, he need not write dully. Joseph Conrad wrote in the preface to *The Nigger of the Narcissus* that the novelist's function was above all to make the reader see, and Purdy's *The Nephew* presents a sober if at times dour vision of life which remains indelibly etched in the reader's mind long after the book has been read.

CHAPTER 4

The Later Stories and Plays: Children Is All

PURDY, having demonstrated with *The Nephew* that he was capable of writing a Realistic novel, next published, in 1961, a collection of ten stories, which had appeared in various magazines in the late 1950s, and two plays in the volume *Children Is All*.[1] As if to indicate that the effort to create fairly normal characters in a Realistic setting in the previous novel may not have been his normal métier and was not in keeping with his real fictional objectives, Purdy returned in these newly collected pieces to the weird, surrealistic world previously portrayed in *Color of Darkness*. Once again, readers were introduced to abnormal and almost hysterical states of consciousness, states which serve as the lens through which to view the manifold infernos in which various characters live. All the characters suffer, to some degree, from the effects of selfishness, lovelessness, loneliness, and alienation; in short, they endure the typical milieu in which Purdy's characters have their being.

Depressing as the content of some of these tales is, Purdy's carefully controlled manner, seemingly effortless prose style, and Realistic speech patterns make four or five of the tales masterpieces in the genre of the grotesque and the bizarre. More important, if excellent writing can be measured by the reverberations created in the readers' minds by the conflicts depicted in these tales, *Children Is All* can be considered to be a worthy successor of *Color of Darkness*.

I The Reality Behind the Facade

However, all of these later narratives are not pervaded with the sense of ominous dread and foreboding that characterized

61

Purdy's earlier stories; in some of them which treat conventional and humdrum situations with no apparent overtones, a vision of hell unexpectedly gapes open below the surface, and we are startled by the abyss before us. Thus, one tale, "Mrs. Benson,"[2] is concerned with nothing more significant than the annual reunion in Paris of Mrs. Benson with her thirty-year-old daughter, Wanda Walters. However, the tale is incandescently illuminated when their talk reverts to an invitation extended many years ago to Wanda's mother, then Rose Walters, and the implications behind the request. The invitation given Rose Walters (soon after her husband had deserted her) by one Mrs. Carlin to come live with her could ordinarily have been interpreted as an act of concern, thoughtfulness and kindness on the part of one woman for another. But as the story unfolds, we learn that the invitation was really an effort on Mrs. Carlin's part to fend off her own loneliness, which was also the result of an unhappy marriage.

Despite the fact that one section of Mrs. Carlin's home had been given over to guests, she could not have cared less for their comfort and entertainment. Instead, she desires to have Rose Walters "stay on," since the others, she tells Rose, are "not for us." Thus she reveals a lack of concern for people, a great degree of selfishness and pride, and perhaps the lesbian overtones which might have led in the first place to her own unhappy marriage. Yet all that Rose Benson remembers of this distant invitation is that she was catered to for a short while by another woman who had also experienced an unhappy marriage. All the while, Rose had never once questioned why some women were either deserted by their husbands or simply had suffered unhappy marriages. Moreover, Rose Benson reveals that she has still not learned the lessons which make for a happy marriage; since Wanda's birth, she has been married and divorced many times.

But then it is apparent that Rose Benson, with her essentially unloving nature, could not have been happy with anyone, let alone with a variety of husbands, when we learn that, during her mature relationship with her daughter Wanda, she has never confided in the girl. And as the mother fondles her many expensive rings during the conversation, we sense the materialism and lovelessness that have governed the thinking of Rose Benson throughout the years. Thus the remark that these "little reunions in Paris are such a pleasure, Mother," creates a chilling effect as we realize that Wanda has not yet achieved the knowledge of her mother that we have.

Similar in its impact to "Mrs. Benson" is a second tale, "About Jessie Mae,"[3] in which the acidic reminiscences of a woman's extraordinary slovenliness are recalled by Myrtle, her distant cousin. We learn that Jessie Mae is indeed slovenly and somewhat malicious, for she leaves her jewelry lying about her house in order to tempt people whom she despises. Because of her essentially honest nature, she is a far better person than either Myrtle or Mrs. Hemlock, in whose immaculate kitchen Myrtle spews forth remembrances of things past to her appropriately named neighbor. Mrs. Hemlock outwardly is an apparently decent woman; in reality, however, she is nothing more than a moral executioner, since she delights in having her beautifully clean kitchen serve as a meeting place where neighbors can drop in to enjoy her ice-box fudge bars. There they verbally lop off the heads of their neighbors as they unload themselves of malicious, poisonous, soul-destroying gossip, which Mrs. Hemlock enjoys hearing.

Totally different in theme and tone from the previous two tales is "Home by Dark,"[4] a parable about the need for faith and about the almost total lack of this intangible yet easily discerned quality in modern man. Centering on an old man and his bright grandson, who is living with him only because the boy's parents are dead, the narrative explores within the period of a couple of hours the hopefulness of a child's dreams; and it reveals through the grandfather's conversation a life that has experienced very little good. Believing that a loose tooth he has saved will turn into a pot of gold the following morning, the boy is encouraged in this belief by the old man because it is a pure wish—and "all wishes like that come true." But before this childish fantasy can be acted upon, the tooth is lost, and efforts to find it prove futile. The disappointments of the grandfather's life are seen at the very end where, unable to comfort the boy, who laments that he does not know what to believe in now that his tooth is gone, the old man can only keep his own

heartbreaking sobs from being heard; and he does this by pushing the boy's head "tight against his breast so [the boy] would
not hear the sounds that came out now like a confused and
trackless torrent. . . ."

Contrived as the plot is, "Home By Dark" is redeemed by
such stylistic effects as the juxtaposition of the grandfather's
faith that a pure wish is always answered with the apparent
failure during his own life to have witnessed this result. Purdy
also uses effectively the constant refrain that, while birds know
enough to be home by dark, man does not have a place to rest
his head in today's world. Especially effective also is the contrast
between the old man's darkened consciousness and the light of
the moon, which makes its appearance at the end of the tale.

Another story that has a grandfather and grandson as two of
its characters is "Night and Day,"[5] but, unlike the grandparent
in "Home By Dark" who is literally both father and mother to
the boy left in his care, Grandy in "Night and Day" wants no
part of his grandchild. All Grandy really wants is Cleo, the boy's
mother, who two years previously suffered the desertion of
Bruce, her husband and Grandy's son. Since then, completely
supported by Grandy, who maintains her apartment, Cleo is
slowly but steadily losing her battle to keep her father-in-law
from possessing her.

Thinking all along that Grandy wanted her to forget and
eliminate Bruce from her life and not his grandson, Cleo finally
realizes that Grandy has no room in his heart for children and
that life with him would be restricted night and day almost exclusively to the bedroom. Startled by the appalling prospect
before her, Cleo summons the strength of character to call
Grandy a "whoring old goat"; with this defiant epithet, Cleo
leaves the impression that she may yet muster the strength of
character to break away from the sexual life Grandy plans for her.

II   *The Grotesque Once More*

In the previous four stories, the major characters may be said
to be normal people, however much they are unaware of their
deficiencies; in the six remaining tales, however, Purdy's penchant for the grotesque is again evident. The reader is presented

with characters whose aberrant and disturbed states of mind cause them untold frustration. When they try to communicate with other people, they fail; when they ask questions, they receive no response. Easily the most poignant of these portrayals of frustration and loneliness is "Daddy Wolf,"[6] an artistic rendering of the plight of a poverty-stricken family who, in the hands of sociologists and welfare workers, would simply have been considered to be another case of the poor who are always with us.

"Daddy Wolf" is essentially the story of Korean War veteran Benny, who has arrived in New York with his wife Mabel and their young son to better their lot. "Daddy Wolf" gains its special impact because, written as a monologue, it permits Benny to reveal the manner in which the economic facts of life have worsted him in his efforts to improve his status. The entire action takes place while Benny is inside a telephone booth and is explaining to a man waiting outside the reason he has been in it so long. Depressed because his wife and son have finally left him, and hungry for help and sympathy, Benny apparently chose a number from the phone book at random; much to his surprise, he found a woman at the other end of the wire who was sympathetic to his tale of woe. Having been accidentally cut off and not knowing the woman's name or number, Benny is in a state of misery "trying to get Operator to re-connect me with a party she just cut me off from. If you're not in a big hurry would you let me just try to get my party again."

What follows is essentially Benny's nervous and hectic recital to the man outside the phone booth of what he had just told the woman over the phone—how he and his family had come to New York and fared decently for a while with the Singer sewing-machine people; but, because of a layoff, he was out of work for six months before he found work at little pay in a factory which manufactured mittens. During the period he was unemployed, Mabel tried to earn some money by engaging in a house-to-house canvassing job; but, when winter arrived, Mabel, with only a thin coat to keep her from the cold, stopped doing this kind of work. So sorely in need was the family for the simple necessities of life that she resorted to prostitution and only ceased this practice when she learned that there had been an unxpectedly large increase in venereal disease in the city. She was so frightened that she took her child and fled from the city, thereby leaving Benny to fend for himself.

We can better appreciate the hardships Benny and his family have had to undergo when we consider the utter squalor that the family had suffered when it first arrived in New York:

When I first moved into this building, . . . I had to pinch myself to be sure I was actually seeing it right, I seen all the dirt before I moved in, but once I was in, I really SEEN: all the traces of the ones who had been here before, people who had died or lost their jobs or found they was the wrong race or something and had had to vacate all of a sudden before they could clean the place up for the next tenant. A lot of them left in such a hurry they just give you a present of some of their belongings and underwear along with their dirt. But then after one party left in such a hurry, somebody else from somewhere moved in, found he could not make it in New York City, and lit out somewhere or maybe was taken to a hospital in a serious condition and never returned.

This filth and Benny's sense of hopelessness are epitomized by the linoleum-covered floors in his apartment. The rats ate holes in the floor "so goddam big that I bet my kid, if he was still here could almost put his leg through the biggest one." Yet when Mabel was with him, life, such as it was, went on for Benny; his cream-of-wheat meal was ready for him in the evening as he returned home from the factory, and kindness was even expressed in this Gehenna by the old man down the hall who made it his business to feed Benny's child the one daily meal that the boy had.

In reaching out for help from these utterly sordid living conditions, Mabel in desperation had telephoned Daddy Wolf, a representative of the kind of agency or institution, which upon hearing the ills or woes of the caller, prescribes certain steps and actions to take to extricate him from his onerous condition. (This phenomenon has become quite popular and almost routine for many Americans in need of help, especially since the end of World War II.) Here these institutions are lampooned in the person of Daddy Wolf; for, when Mabel calls him on the "trouble phone" and reveals the reasons she has engaged in prosititution, all Daddy Wolf can tell her is that she should attend church, devote herself to her husband's needs, and stay away from other men.

What is so repugnant is that Daddy Wolf is merely a symbol of the spiritual barrenness of our times in which the pressures and ills of modern life are to be removed, so to speak, by a telephone call to some self-appointed spiritual counselor whose cheery but stereotyped message of hope will be enough to solve the problems of some people's unfortunate living conditions. Moreover, Daddy Wolf's inadequate response reminds us of Graitop's cheerful sense of religion in "Plan Now to Attend," where the former atheist had no real sense of religion with which to help people. In a similar sense, Daddy Wolf's inane remarks exhibit no real religious conviction when he is called upon to help. Thus Benny's cry at the end, "This here is an emergency phone call, Operator," is altogether heartrending. For, in a world without an understanding God or a religion that can aid man, man does confront an emergency when sympathetic people who will listen are cut off from the one seeking assistance. In having told the story of a couple and their child who combat poverty and squalor and of their inevitable defeat by the social and economic forces of our day, Purdy in a mere nine pages has illuminated the bestial conditions in which thousands of Americans still live in the ghettoes of our large cities and has simultaneously fashioned a work of art from some of the most repellent aspects of human life.

Similar to "Daddy Wolf" in its theme of frustration and loneliness is "Everything Under the Sun,"[7] an account of two youths —Jesse, who is twenty, and Cade, who is five years younger. Both share a dingy room in some large city. In Purdy's fiction, the geographical area is unimportant since he is interested only in the states of consciousness entertained by his characters. That no better room can be obtained is evidently the result of Cade's inability or unwillingness to find a job. This unemployment galls Jesse, who finds it takes all his meager earnings to support them. Jesse supports Cade, we learn, because of a sense of duty; for during the war Cade's brother had saved Jesse's life and, in the effort, had lost his own. Maintaining Cade, however, would not have become intolerable, we sense, had not Jesse recently "gotten religion." As a result, some of the practices, such as drinking, smoking, and whoring, that he and Cade had previously enjoyed have become repugnant to him.

The fact is, however, that Jesse has not come by his conversion in a rational and understanding manner. His newly found faith has not made him a larger and more expansive person; instead, he has become somewhat of a fanatic and a man who still does not know himself, if he ever did. As Cade perceptively points out about their two personalities, "I may be dumb, but I'm all together." Thus, when Jesse, in a moment of anger, suggests he and Cade sever their relationship permanently, he is appalled when Cade takes him at his word and leaves. But he does not leave for long, for Jesse is far more in need of human companionship and the younger boy's clear-sightedness than he realizes. Thus, when called back, Cade, in an O'Henry type of ending, now informs Jesse that drink and women are back "in" since, as Cade sees his friend's need, "You need me to tell you who you are." Here we are reminded of *The Nephew*, where Willard Parker is also dominated by the fear that his young friend Vernon Miller may leave him. The special impact left by the two protagonists in "Everything Under the Sun" is that the feelings and instincts of the natural man Cade are far better guides to normal living than is Jessie's hasty conversion. The latter experience would rid him of certain fleshly habits before sufficient spiritual regeneration had had an adequate opportunity to make him a better man.

A tale with an altogether different theme is "Encore,"[8] for it reveals a mother-son relationship. Merta, the frustrated mother, wants nothing more for her son Gibbs, who has been born out of wedlock, than that he be successful in college. To her, college success means hobnobbing and becoming friendly with the rich boys and girls. However, Gibbs makes it clear that, to be popular with rich students, he would also have had to come from an affluent family. Clear-sighted as Gibbs's view is, this announcement has a shattering effect on Merta, who has done nothing but work for years in a factory to accumulate the money to place Gibbs in college.

Plain-looking, middle-aged, and the kind of woman no man would look at twice, Merta is a completely thwarted person; but, even more galling to her at this point is the fact that Gibbs, while unable to make friends with the moneyed cliques at school, has become friendly with Spyro, the son of a Greek restaurant owner in the town. This friendship with a boy from the working class, the social class she wishes to repudiate by providing a college education for her son, is the final blow. She is finally reduced to asking Gibbs to tell her what she needs to do to make her apartment more attractive so that college boys and girls will want to visit him there. So pathetic and hungry is she now for her boy's success in any way possible that, when he wishes to earn a living playing the harmonica, she approves. She previously had thought of the instrument as a mere toy.

Struggling "to keep the storm within her quiet, the storm that now if it broke might sweep everything within her away," Merta is the epitome of nervous despair; and she is at the point of hysteria as she keeps requesting encores from her son, who has started to play the harmonica in her presence. Even more rankling deep down than Gibbs's choice of a vocation is her realization that her relationship with her boy is based on sand. For, in his attempt to kiss her, she remembered that he did it in a manner "resembling someone surreptitiously spitting out a seed."

Readjustment to a scale of values lower than those she had visualized for Gibbs is Merta's sad fate as a mother; readjustment is also the fate visited upon Polly, the slow-witted, sixteen-year-old girl in "The Lesson,"[9] who has become sexually awakened to Mr. Diehl, the handsome swimming instructor who works at the pool owned by Polly's grandmother. While the plot centers on an argument between Polly and Mr. Diehl over whether or not some woman should be allowed to use the pool at the same hour that the swimming instructor had reserved it for a private session, "The Lesson" is really concerned with Polly's desire to have the instructor become sexually aware of her. To achieve this end, Polly, while arguing for the woman's right to use the pool at the same time that he is to give his lesson, edges closer to Mr. Diehl; for she is completely mesmerized by his well-developed biceps and by the water falling from his chest onto her blouse. He, of course, as would be expected, is all the while completely unaware of the effect of his physical presence upon the girl.

Still Polly is motivated by more than just getting close to him and thus fulfilling her budding sexual fantasies. As she sees the situation, Mr. Diehl has for too long had things his own way. Thus, in not consenting to his request that she refuse the woman the use of the pool, Polly is seeking to defeat him at least on this point. Noticing, too, how uncomfortable he has become when, in the course of the quarrel, she lays her hands on his arms and keeps them there, she becomes elated at his discomfiture. Exasperated at his inability to convert Polly to his way of thinking about the use of the pool and roughly removing her hands from his arms, Mr. Diehl has the surprise of his life when, in her nervous sexual desire, Polly butts him into the pool; and, in so doing, she falls in herself. By this time, however, the girl's fantasies are over. Having swallowed great gulps of water and having been given artificial respiration by him, she has had her fill of Mr. Diehl. "Don't lean over me, please, and let the water fall from you on me. Please, please go back into the pool. I don't want you close now. Go back into the pool." While the narrative seems a bit contrived, the attempt to picture a young girl's budding sexual awareness is highly successful in that it gives the impression that young girls naturally react in this fashion to men who have attracted them.

Where sexual ambivalence had been the theme of "The Lesson," "Goodnight, Sweetheart"[10] is a study of the sexual violation of Pearl Miranda, a sixty-year-old elementary schoolteacher, who is described in the opening line as walking down the street at night "stark naked from her classroom." While this description is an example of Purdy at his shocking best, the description is not meant to titillate the reader but to make him aware of the reason for this extraordinary behavior. Having been raped in her classroom late that afternoon, Pearl had had her clothes taken from her by the rapist; and this incident accounts for her nudeness. Literally the victim of the "blackboard-jungle" way of life, Pearl had been assaulted by the brother of a thirteen-year-old girl whom she had been previously instrumental in having sent to the reformatory for whorish behavior. Ironically enough, Pearl's reward for having testified against the girl's sexual aberration is being raped in revenge by the girl's older brother when she is alone in her classroom.

Still, Pearl Miranda is not altogether blameless, we feel, for what has happened to her. As with most of Purdy's characters, she appears alienated from the mainstream of life, for she spends most of her days in the schoolroom and has few interests outside it. Thus it seems psychologically right that the home Pearl seeks to enter after her assault belongs to Winston Cramer, who had been one of her students some twenty years previously. Now nearly thirty-three and a piano teacher, Winston is also an estranged character, and lives alone in the house left him by his deceased mother. There he spends his days endeavoring to teach ungifted children to play the piano.

Once recovered from the initial shock of seeing Pearl standing nude before him, Winston robes her; but he is unable to accept the horrible truth of her sexual assault. Taking to his bed to regain his mental and physical composure, Winston advises Pearl to do the same since she has become chilled as a result of her previous exposure to the night air. In the last scene, Pearl has been urged to go to bed and to rest if possible; Winston, unable to leave her, lies next to her. Here is a perfect example of estrangement come full circle. She, literally in a state of incipient shock because of what had happened to her at her age, can only keep moaning "God, Oh God"; he, only wishing to help her, bids her "Goodnight, sweetheart"; but nothing really exists between them to evoke his phrase of endearment.

What makes "Goodnight, Sweetheart" so effective, in addition to the bizarre events already noted, is the validity of its opening scene. The rape of Pearl Miranda in the George Washington School where she teaches has been duplicated in real life in various areas of the United States and several times in New York City schools where any motive for revenge on the part of the raper was not even present. Further heightening the appeal of this narrative is that the reader is once again presented with the problem of determining whether Pearl and Winston are white or black, but the style is hauntingly evocative of the Negro idiom and character. Whether or not the tale is about blacks, the theme is universal and can relate to any race or nationality anywhere.

Without a doubt, one of the most provocative pieces in *Children Is All* is "Sermon,"[11] which is not a story but a four-page essay, the content of which resembles Jonathan Edwards's "Sinners in the Hands of an Angry God" as it might read in our time. Edwards wrote his sermon in the hope of regenerating the lives of his parishioners, but Purdy's "Sermon" does not extend hope for twentieth-century man. If the speaker can be equated with God, then twentieth-century man is in a spiritual hell that even Edwards's Puritan theology never conceived. For, although the Puritan theology viewed man as totally depraved, it always contained the sense of the irresistible grace of God, one which was capable of redeeming any sinner who sought redemption. Purdy's "Sermon" holds no such hope for mankind, for since all of "you came originally wrong," "there is, in fact, no hope for you and there never was." To add insult to injury, God himself admits that he is "a mistake, and how could my coming be a success."

On another level, one of affirmation, God hints that had mankind, to use the Aristotelian phrase, "become" instead of having just existed, the situation might have been much better for the world. But the steps to gain this desirable end are not divulged, and we feel that God does not really wish to release man from the yoke of original sin that He has fastened on him after Adam and Eve lost Eden. So vigorous and contemporary is the indictment of mankind's present morass that, however "Sermon" may be interpreted by its readers, it commands their attention because of the cogency of the ideas presented.

III *The Plays*: Cracks *and* Children Is All

The pessimistic view of life in the tales is also characteristic of the two plays that Purdy has written, *Children Is All* and *Cracks*, both of which are short pieces. At present, Purdy need not fear that his services as a dramatist will be in great demand, since paradoxically enough, while the dialogue is excellent and the plots are logically worked out, the ominous mood which suffuses his best stories and gives them their particular flavor is practically absent from the plays. This characteristic is particularly true of *Cracks*,[12] which depends for much of its effect on its two main characters, Nera, an eighty-year-old widow, and a second shadowy figure, who is referred to as the Creator. In one sense, *Cracks* continues along the same thematic line as "Sermon," but in a more hopeful vein. Portrayed awaiting death, Nera has learned, as a result of her experiences, to ask some of the important questions. Once the mother of four children, all of whom had died before reaching maturity, and the wife of an embezzler who had left her, Nera simply does not believe that this temporal life in which she has been immersed all these years is the be-all and end-all of existence. To her, it is inconceivable that the pain of birth results eventually in nothing more than death. In challenging this idea, the Creator informs her that a frightful noise that has been heard signifies the end of the world. But, when Nera perseveres in her affirmation of an afterlife that makes restitution for the tribulations suffered in this temporal one, the Creator is forced to admit that the explosion he set off to end the world has not succeeded. For, once the world He created was set in motion, it became something more than the Creator could control and had to continue by its very nature.

Although the theme of questioning the nature of the universe is vital and affirmative, it is difficult to see how the play could have been a success, since it has very little action and is merely a long dialogue about immortality versus mortality. Interspersed are such clichés as the dead are soon forgotten by those who live on and there is no love in the world. In its own way, however, *Cracks* serves as an antidote to the negativism expressed in "Sermon."

"Children Is All"[13] is more powerful as a theatrical work than *Cracks*. The title is derived from a remark made by Edna Cartwright, the chief character, about the noise made by children who are shooting fireworks on July 4, the day the events in the play occur. A previous use of a national holiday as a backdrop for a narrative was the Memorial Day setting in *The Nephew*; but, significantly, where Cliff is the nephew who was loved by his aunt and uncle before he went to Korea to die, lack of affection in *Children Is All* literally sends Edna Cartwright's son, Billy, the thirty-five-year-old jailbird to his death on Inde-

pendence Day—as if to signify his intention to be free of a
life in which he had been rejected from birth.

For, in one sense, Edna Cartwright epitomizes the apex of
childishness characteristic of Purdy's many adults who, because
of their own immaturity, wreak havoc with the lives of their
children. In this sense, Edna Cartwright is a typically unloving
Purdian parent; for, after having married young and having lost
her husband shortly thereafter, she deeply resented having to
rear her child alone. Now nearly fifty and living in her own home
with Leona Khetchum as a companion, Edna as the play opens
remembers only too well that Billy, when he was twenty years
old and working in a bank, stole some money and was consequently sentenced to fifteen years in prison. That she never got
close to her boy as he grew up, or that Billy actually served as
the "fall guy" for the officers in the bank who were the real
culprits, had no significance for Edna, to whom respectability
and outward conformity are the central tenets of her being. To
her, it was sufficient that her boy, who had been accused of
stealing money, had therefore disgraced her.

These memories are stirred because, having served his sentence, Billy is at last returning home, a circumstance Edna cannot face, since she has never visited him in the state penitentiary.
She had made trips for that purpose at first, but, confronted with
the necessity of entering the forbidding prison walls, she had
lost heart and after a while had simply stopped going. Now after
a fifteen-year hiatus, she is confronted with the exigency of her
son's homecoming.

To contrast Edna's withdrawal from and rejection of her son,
Purdy presents the care, thoughtfulness, and love that a teen-
ager has begun to show toward Billy. Illegitimate Hilda, who
has been reared by Uncle Ben, one of Edna's next-door neighbors, has just turned eighteen. During the previous year she had
made several trips to the penitentiary to cheer Billy up. Edna,
however, is so deeply disturbed by the ordeal of having her
son return home after all these years that she actually faints
away. Not entirely unexpectedly, Edna, at the close of day and
alone in her parlor in a comatose condition because of her
turbulent feelings, actually refuses to acknowledge Billy when he
appears with an ugly wound in his temple. She cries, "No, no,

you're not him! Billy was only a boy"; and, cleaving still to the past, she forgoes the present with its possibility for reconciliation and forgiveness. Also demeaning to Edna, who cares only for appearances, is the fact that she is a liar who refuses to face the truth. For Billy's wound, which soon proves fatal, is the result of his having broken out of prison. Edna, who knows about such attempts to escape, appears to be unaware of them, for she does not wish to acknowledge that her son is a convict.

Efforts to make Edna realize that Billy has come home solely to be acknowledged as her son before he dies are of no avail; for, although people like Hilda and Leona Khetchum can "see" and thus accept Billy because of their total acceptance of life, Edna simply cannot, or refuses to, do so. Thus Billy's last anguished utterance that his mother remain "blind" best summarizes the utter futility of his life as a son who was never really seen or accepted. Aside from her refusal to acknowledge Billy, Edna is still holding fast to respectability as the cardinal tenet of her being, a fact best indicated in her sarcastic remark to Hilda that no "fatherless little bastard" need remind her of her duties as a mother. This outburst takes place after Hilda implores Edna to act as a mother to Billy, an action which Edna refuses to take. In fact, only after Billy dies does she feel close to him; for in death Billy is no longer present to serve as a deterrent to her sense of propriety. Edna is, therefore, quite unlike Alma in *The Nephew*, who finally realizes that the love she bore her nephew had been returned. Alma can remain happy in that knowledge, but only by Billy's dying can Edna find comfort that a convict in the guise of her son is no longer around to disturb her sense of decorum.

While *Children Is All* is a far more interesting play than *Cracks*, "Cracks" was chosen—together with "Everything Under the Sun," "Encore," "Sermon," "Don't Call Me by My Right Name," and "You Reach for Your Hat"—to be adapted for the stage. Cast into dramatic form by Ellen Violett and staged under the title of *Color of Darkness: An Evening in the World of James Purdy* in New York at the Writer's Stage on September 30, 1963, the six pieces received no better press than Albee's adaptation of *Malcolm* later received in January, 1966. As Lewis Funke of the *New York Times* noted,[14] the empathy which a reader could achieve in a quiet room with the author's work, as well as the mood created by this sympathetic sense, was not easily re-created in the theater. While acknowledging Purdy's power as a writer and his sensitivity of spirit, Funke observed that, in the adaptation of the stories to the theater, the end product was not drama but a series of talking stage pictures. And, while each tale had its moment of truth, dramatic impact was lacking; instead, all the plays had the effect of a series of vignettes whose characters appeared to be no stronger than shadows.

Although Purdy's fiction did not lend itself successfully to the stage, the collection of tales in *Children Is All* did receive in the main a complimentary press as fiction. Old admirers praised the new work and some critics who were reviewing him for the first time also found much in his latest work that they considered worthy. One of the old admirers, Ihab Hassan, who had referred to Purdy as "a promising newcomer" in *Radical Innocence*, his study of the contemporary American novel, found this promise now confirmed and bade readers to rejoice in the possession of this new work by "one of America's best writers."[15] Winfield Townley Scott, who had also followed Purdy's career from the outset, welcomed the new volume; and he found in various stories those elements of good fiction which had made the author "the exciting writer he has been from the first."[16]

On the other hand, William Peden, also an early Purdy enthusiast who had been lavish in his praise of Purdy's earlier fiction, found the writing in *Children Is All* to be "lacking the fierce and shocking impact of the stories in *Color of Darkness.*" Compensating for this deficiency was the author's concern with the bizarre and the unusual; and this bent, as well as the world and the situation from which they emerged, was more immediately recognized in *Children Is All.*[17] Benjamin DeMott also found the gifts displayed in the new volume to be not so forceful as in the previous works, but he thought that Purdy had unmistakable gifts as a writer.[18] The impeccable control over his material which DeMott regarded as one of Purdy's strong points had also impressed Guy Davenport, who, while admiring Purdy's ability, observed that nowhere in the new volume had the author "found a theme worthy of his technique."[19] Also negative in his review was Robert Taubman, who found at times that the many human failures of communication portrayed in the tales tended to reach the level of fantasy; and, while the author had more literary resourcefulness than other young American writers, Taubman thought that such resourcefulness was evidently needed since the material did not have the feel "of being firsthand and hard won."[20]

Negative comments, such as those found in the reviews of Davenport and Taubman, were few and far between. Instead, the favorable review by Irving Malin of the new volume was indicative of most reviewers' reactions. Pointing out that Purdy's fiction most powerfully dramatized the fantastic, Malin asserted that not only did Purdy "give us deep truth" in his "disconcertingly original" stories but he also had more to say about American civilization than did the novels, for example, of John Updike.[21] This was rather high praise for an author who had so far written only four books; but on the basis of the various indictments Purdy had hitherto made of certain American institutions and ideals, Malin's observation was not far wrong. The question now was whether Purdy could combine in one piece of fiction the various satirical thrusts that he had previously portrayed in disparate fashion in *Color of Darkness, Malcolm,* and *Children Is All.*

Were he capable of doing so, there was ample material at hand; for, by the middle of the highly technological and impersonal 1960s, a spokesman was needed to depict the basic immorality and shallowness of a way of life that was based on nothing more substantial than material and economic success. In short, the time was ripe for *Cabot Wright Begins,* which is perhaps Purdy's most important work so far because of its trenchant portrayal of American life in the last half of our century.

CHAPTER 5

Novels of Satire and of Love: Cabot Wright Begins and Eustace Chisholm and The Works

"OUR culture is based on money and competition. It is inhuman, terrified of love, sexual and other, and obsessed with homosexuality and brutality. Our entire life is pestiferous; we live in an immoral atmosphere." Far from being the censures of some pessimistic and cynical sociologist, these animadversions are Purdy's; and they appear on the blurb of his third novel, *Cabot Wright Begins* which was published in the fall of 1964.[1] But, since Purdy is not a sociologist but a storyteller, he must present his truths in the form of fiction, which he does in *Cabot Wright Begins*. The novel may be remembered in the future not so much for its story line, however, as for its excoriating, vitriolic attack on American society and on some of its more important institutions in this half of the twentieth century. In fact, Purdy is so deeply hostile in his indictment of our way of life that we are reminded of the satires of Sinclair Lewis. But, where Lewis in *Main Street* and *Babbitt* scored the narrow-minded, petty, and complacent small-town life of the Middle-west of the 1920s, Purdy has taken to task our whole highly developed, technological civilization; and he focuses his diatribe on urban America in general and on New York City in particular, which is the setting of his novel.

For insight into the kind of life most Americans lived during the 1960s, *Cabot Wright Begins* will no doubt become the American counterpart to a great degree of Jonathan Swift's *Gulliver's Travels*; for it reveals to students of sociology that, although some two hundred and fifty years separate these

78

satires, the follies and stupidities of mankind remain perpetual, regardless of the society or century involved.

This being so, the plot, which is only a device to set forth the satire, need not concern us unduly, revolving as it does around the efforts of several people to obtain the life story of Cabot Wright, a twenty-six-year-old stockbroker turned rapist. Each person has his reasons for the quest; and one of them is to make money by publishing Wright's life as fiction.[2] Among these seekers of Cabot's story are Bernie Gladhart, a former used-car salesman turned writer; Zoe Bickle, a friend of Bernie's and of his wife, Carrie Moore, and a literary agent in her own right; and Princeton Keith, a publisher's scout who seriously needs a story that will sell well. As they get at the truth of Cabot's radical change, the reader is exposed to scenes of corruption, dehumanization, and alienation which unfortunately are not only true but also have become more and more the mise-en-scène of American life in our time. Farcical as it may seem, the reason Cabot, basically a decent person, turns rapist, as E. M. Forster would put it, is simply "to connect"; for he finds his social milieu barren, lifeless, and unreal.

Cabot is bored working on Wall Street; his real love is the world of art, the subject he had majored in while at Yale. And, since a Madison Avenue publisher is eagerly interested in Cabot's illicit sexual career for the tremendous windfall the strory would bring him, both the financial and publishing industries come under careful scrutiny and are scathingly portrayed. Current malaises, problems, and abuses—race relations, television commercials, and medical charlatanism—are also trenchantly depicted. However, Wall Street and Madison Avenue are essentially the bêtes noires of Purdy's satire. Since Cabot returns to New York in order to hide after his release from prison, it is altogether fitting that this mecca of brokerage and publishing houses serves as the backdrop of the novel.

I *New York City as Background*

From the opening scene, which finds Bernie Gladhart, recently removed from Chicago, walking along the Promenade in Brooklyn Heights and looking out at night across the East

River to the dark caverns of Wall Street, there is an air of verisimilitude to the description for anyone who knows this area of the city. Purdy has completely absorbed the atmosphere of this neighborhood, and especially the Joralimon Street section in which Bernie believes Cabot has gone into hiding. The atmosphere reeks with the squalor, blight, and dinginess which the drifters and the low-income groups who live there have given it. Yet Bernie is so intent on hunting down Cabot that he is oblivious to the surroundings, a fact that serves to heighten the squalor around him. And by referring to the See-River Manor, the apartment house where Bernie lives, as the Cockroach Palace, Purdy makes the scene appear even more noisome than it is.

Other places in New York whose atmosphere Purdy has captured include such localities and landmarks as Central Park, 42nd Street, lower Broadway, Red Hook, Hanover Square, and especially the Brooklyn Bridge, over which Cabot walks daily from his apartment in Brooklyn Heights to his office in Wall Street. This daily stroll seems to be the only activity he really enjoys before he becomes alienated from American life of the 1960s.

II *Wall Street as a Way of Life*

The reason Cabot rapes over three hundred women and girls, nearly all of whom seemingly do not resist him, is the complete and utter boredom that Cabot experiences in his Wall Street position.[3] Furthermore, Cabot rapes, as he puts it, the "dumbest dames" he can find, as if he seeks to intensify the ennui from which he constantly suffers because of his activities as a broker. Rape, he claims, is the only joy left him[4] since "pleasure died 40 years ago in America, perhaps further back, in a wave of carbon monoxide, gasoline, cigarettes for dames, the belief in everything and everybody, tolerance for the intolerable, the hatred of being alone in silence for more than 20 seconds. . . ."[5]

Thus, for Cabot, the art major at Yale who had been shunted into a high-paying Wall Street position by his rich foster-father, becoming a rapist is merely symptomatic, we deduce, of the rape of the mind that transpires in contemporary life. Man's aspirations for more esthetic, soul-satisfying work literally surrender under pressure to merely monetary rewards; but, in Cabot's case, the quest for real fulfillment fulminates in rape.

If the selling of stocks and bonds is anathema to Cabot, this occupation is literally meat and drink to Warburton, Cabot's boss. Warburton, a latter-day Babbitt, is a caricature of Daddy Warbucks of the *Little Orphan Annie* comic strip, who has for years epitomized all that is rugged and virile among modern American corporate tycoons. Warburton is one of four partners whose surnames of Slider, Bergler, and Gorem denote their specific economic and social propensities; but Warburton would find his life a total vacuum if he were deprived of his daily opportunity to engage in the shady financial transactions which have already netted him enormous wealth. Warburton is presented with great gusto and Dickensian vividness of character; and, like some of Dickens's caricatures, he represents some of the worst character traits that are almost always allied with great greed and with monetary success.

To encourage Cabot and to "sell" him on the Wall Street way of life, Warburton cites the need to get on the winning team—the capitalists—since this group will decide the future. In short, Warburton is the complete expression of a culture whose sole raison d'être is the making and the accumulating of financial fortunes. So devoid is he of other interests that when he makes a fortune, his first concern is to double it immediately.[6] That a person's capacities and talents might be spent on interests other than the accumulation of wealth seems altogether madness to him. Yet he is perceptive enough to note that the gospel of wealth that he lives by has not appealed to the bulk of his fellow citizens. This realization leads him to the writing of what he calls "sermons" which are in reality blistering diatribes against everything and everybody, including himself. These sermons are meant solely for Warburton's private use, for his reflections are so bitter that we imagine that he would have been dismissed from the hallowed halls of capitalism had a fellow tycoon read them. The sermons constitute Purdy's attack on the shoddy values and practices of contemporary life, and these diatribes are set forth with the primary intent of shocking the reader and awakening him from his apathy so that he will rectify the conditions Purdy criticizes.

Cabot somehow managed to get hold of the sermons and to read them while he served his prison sentence. Understanding the underlying reasons for the corruption that Warburton's diatribes reveal, Cabot is cured of his raping instinct. Significantly enough, Warburton manages to note that the excesses committed by the magnates of big business in their unrelenting pursuit of profits are just those that have led to some of the worst ravages of the individuality and dignity of their fellow Americans. Furthermore, as one of these magnates, he begins to realize his responsibility for the barrenness of love and joy that pervades the American scene as a result of this inordinate desire for wealth.

III   Satire—American Style

Not a single important area of modern life is spared in Warburton's indictments. Again, so hostile in tone are they that the impression gained, by and large, is that most Americans are latter-day Yahoos, animalistic to the core. Even more numbing is the realization that—look where we will in this land of the fee and the home of the knave—we will find very few Houyhnhnms available in the last third of this century to serve as models of rationality for their benighted brethren. Thus the contemporary scene is portrayed as a hallucinatory nightmare of fraud, imbecility, sexual frustration, and violence. All of these conditions and states of mind reach their climax, as it were, in the way most Americans eat. To Americans, the devouring of countless hamburgers and bags of popcorn either in moviehouses or in front of their television sets is simply the way people eat. That dining may take place on a higher level is not even thought of.

To show that good sense is no longer part of the American scene, Warburton contrasts the welding of the original thirteen colonies into a more perfect union as a perfectly rational act on the part of the Founding Fathers; modern America is viewed, however, as nothing more than a jazzed-up, meretricious civilization. This fact is exemplified by thousands of salesmen who are busily selling all kinds of goods at any price to ordinary citizens who are subjected to an unrelenting pressure to buy products they do not really need.

Particularly heinous to Warburton—as an example of the corruption that has eroded our moral fiber—are the faces in the Miss Subway ads. He sees the winsome young ladies portrayed in them as middle-aged women wearing wigs; even worse is the fact that, regardless of their age, all of these ladies are ready to engage in illicit sex to advance their careers,[7] a situation somewhat analogous to that in Edward Albee's *Everything in the Garden* in which suburban housewives work as prostitutes in their spare time in order to make some extra money. Another example of Warburton's complete disgust with the tasteless advertising of big business is his vision of the sale of a certain brand of toilet paper after a beautiful actress will have been seen by millions on television using it to wipe her anus. At this point, the excessive emphasis placed on illicit sex and on the ordinary functions of the body reminds us of Swift's use of these and gives credence to Frederick Crews's comment that the facts of human nature seem to nauseate Purdy, who mistakes his nausea for social criticism.[8]

But, if Warburton's indictment of the methods employed by big business and advertising firms is bitter, even more caustic are his evaluations of his fellow Americans. American men are depicted as unsure of their sexual prowess, an insecurity that leads them to be seen in public with women rather than with other men. And, while American males are presented as little more than faggots, American women are "dyed-in-the-wool irregular anaesthetic whores."[9] This anaesthesia, Warburton notes, is a condition widespread in American life; Cabot is evidently the embodiment of this phenomenon, we are told, since he emerged without feeling from his mother's womb.[10]

To reinforce his view that this lack of feeling is native to most Americans in our day, Purdy creates the scene in which Cabot, as he wanders aimlessly across town, hears an evangelist telling her audience that Americans are so bloated with sin that they do wrong because of boredom rather than because of a desire for adventure. For leadership to guide them out of this Slough of Despond, those who should be qualified to do so, the Presidents, are of no help; for at bottom everything, even the Presidency, is motivated by the almighty dollar: the moneycup has displaced the buttercup as the favorite flower of the land.[11] Even the wealthy, whom the tycoon once remembered as being people of character, come off badly at Warburton's hands; for, shown as immersed in creature comforts and pleasures, they have absolutely no idea of noblesse oblige.

No less vehement are Warburton's arraignments against such institutions as the medical profession, organized religion, and television, with its pernicious influence. According to Warburton, the practice of medicine nowadays is largely a fraud. We are given the case of one Dr. Bigelow-Martin, previously known as Bugleford, who, because of malpractice, was forced to change his name and leave Brooklyn Heights for Lower Broadway. In his practice, Dr. Martin is seen giving two patients with distinctly different ailments the same advice—to relax. Making this advice seem humorously inappropriate to Warburton, who happened to be one of the patients, was the knowledge of what would happen if he even dared to follow Martin's seemingly innocent counsel: "Once ... deprived of tenseness and anger, his business empire would crumble—he would be calm and happy and penniless."[12]

Martin's charlatanism is similar to that engaged in by doctors in the novels of John Barth and Saul Bellow, and Purdy's portrayal reflects the small degree of respect such quacks have lately been given. Another healing agency, organized religion, does not fare well in the portrayal of Reverend Cross, whom Cabot comes to know after his release from jail. Represented as a young man who "suffered from spiritual diseases of his own, as witness circles under his eyes, rapid pulse ... looking at boys' crotches,"[13] Reverend Cross is a caricature; at the same time, he is the embodiment of all that is ineffectual and traditional in religion—for he lacks the vigor, idealism, and joy we expect from a person deeply committed to uplifting spiritual values. Thus his advice that Cabot live righteously falls on deaf ears; and Cabot's repudiation of Reverend Cross's ethos is understandable, since he considers the minister's advice to be nothing more than "Daddy-rattling and pious alarm."

Not so very long ago the whole area of television was labeled a wasteland; and Warburton sees this medium as devoted solely to the idea of "sex-unsex." Again, the deeply narcotic effect television has on its viewers is seen in the remark that Tuesday evenings are for some people their "gaze-nights." As for the related medium of radio and the incessant caterwauling to be heard over its many stations, Warburton terms this drivel "Jewish-Negro hot-box music," and his criticism ends there.

One of the social ills not inveighed against by Warburton's sermons is the emphasis Americans place on youthfulness and on the need of forever looking young. This malaise, however, is closely allied to his major indictments and gives rise to one of the more titillating episodes in the novel—Cabot's successive rapes of Zenda Stuyvesant, a retired middle-aged movie star, and her teenaged daughter Goldie. Zenda is shown as not so much concerned that her own honor and dignity have been violated as she is about Goldie, who earns her living as a model. Nor is the daughter's thinking much loftier than her mother's; for, already eighteen but posing as a sixteen-year old when modeling, Goldie is not concerned that she has lost her chastity; she merely wonders if her rape may have terminated her modeling career.

Zenda and Goldie lack a true sense of values, so when they begin to reflect on their sexual violations, the effect is hilarious. When Zenda pleads with Cabot prior to his rape of Goldie that since he is a member of a profession and can appreciate what "one thing of this kind" can do, he should appreciate the fact that Goldie has to perpetually look like a "sweet sixteen" model if she is to remain employed.[14] All told, the blistering satire leveled at these aspects of contemporary society and thought appears to be even more valid now than it was nearly a decade ago when Purdy made his indictment.

However, the total impact of the attack is marred because Purdy permits his contempt of certain practices and vices to destroy momentarily the firm control that he normally exerts over his material. As a result, the exposé loses some of the force that a more restrained approach would have obtained. Still, *Cabot Wright Begins* is to a great degree a twentieth-century duplicate of *Gulliver's Travels*, but our brands of follies

and stupidities are even more despicable than those Swift lashed
at in his day. In a similar sense, Purdy's caustic portrayal of the
New York literary establishment within the larger picture of
his satire can also be viewed as an updated version of the
flailing that another English satirist, Alexander Pope, gave his
literary foes in *The Dunciad.*

IV   *Of Books and Critics*

Purdy's setbacks in getting his early works published in the
United States have already been discussed; eventually, his
hostility toward certain publishers and literary critics whom
he felt to be instrumental in rejecting him was bound to erupt.
When it did so in *Cabot Wright Begins,* no one suffered more
from Purdy's belated rancor than Alfred Knopf. The portrait of
tycoon Al Guggelhaupt is as devastating a caricature as we will
find in the annals of the publishing industry. Because of his
German ancestry, Guggelhaupt is portrayed as a bully who
exhibits traits similar to those previously expressed by two
Teutonic aggrandizers, Bismarck and Kaiser Wilhelm. When
first introduced to the reader, the publisher is already the
philistine owner of the Goliath Publishing House. His obtuse
literary values are expressed in his current edict to his chief
editor, Princeton Keith, to find a new book, any book, for
publication or suffer the company's early retirement plan.

Not that Keith, the "Jehovah in New York publishing," has
not made wads of money for his boss, who sees himself as the
Goethe of publishers. Interestingly enough, all this money has
come from the sale of best sellers, a fact that Keith, a man of
artistic values, presently bemoans. Having been pressured by
his boss through the years, Keith has lowered his sights. Therefore, in an age of "poop," as his friend Zoe Bickle puts it, best
sellers are the only kind of books that make money; and the
word has gone forth that he must publish a new book or
"retire." To this end Keith enlists the aid of Zoe, a former
literary editor herself, not only to edit the manuscript which
Bernie Gladheart has written about Cabot's life but to see
whether she can obtain any related information from Wright
himself.

Keith is intent upon getting the former rapist's life in print because of his boss's insistence that the reading public is currently ripe for a book about rape. Having begun as a publisher of erotica in the 1920s, Guggelhaupt is shown as still pursuing this bent, where he insists that Keith make the book on "Wright right," that is, as salacious as possible.[15] But, if the publisher is opportunistic and greedy, neither is Keith an angel. Having sold out his values, he is shown as the kind of editor who can discover a good writer and then work like mad to prevent his getting published; in short, Keith is the kind of man who typifies "America in action—opposed to quality."[16]

But, after Keith has readied the manuscript about Wright for publication, his boss becomes doubtful of its suitability and decides to have it read by various critics, including his wife Corinna. At this point Purdy's vindictiveness against various reviewers becomes his vengeance. *Indelible Smudge*, as the manuscript is titled, is first of all denounced by Corinna, who views it as entirely out of tune with the literary Zeitgeist. Consequently, she contends, it would not meet with the approval of Tim Raisin (Alfred Kazin, no doubt), the leading reviewer among those critics inclined to the left.[17] Another critic, Talcum Downley (Malcolm Cowley, to be sure), is credited with having discovered the Flat-Foot School of Writers (the late Jack Kerouac and the other Beats) and is made to appear to be a mental nonentity. He finds *Indelible Smudge* morally reprehensible, since to him the only suitable themes worthy of American fiction, are war and military life. Moreover, because there are too few good current novels, and because all of them are thin in quantity, Downley proposes that writers "bring back bloat into the novel"; they are to do so by remembering that "the only subject a real American novel must always and perforce touch on is war.[18] Still another critic, Cordell Bicks, "the great pink critic of the Thirties" (who else but Granville Hicks?), insists that rape as a literary theme has been a dead one for several years.[19]

The one critic that Purdy really knifes is Orville Prescott, who until a few years ago was one of the most influential and powerful literary critics of our time. Depicted as a nincompoop who espouses God, motherhood, and apple pie as suitable themes for fiction, Doyley Pepscout has no objection to rape as a legitimate subject for a novel; he deplores, however, the fact that the rapist is not shown to be in contact with the many happy people who daily surround him. To Pepscout, *Indelible Smudge*, instead of presenting the smiling aspects of American life a la William Dean Howells, is merely a study in degeneracy. Prescott knew that he was the target of Purdy's verbal knife thrust, for the tone of his short review of *Cabot Wright Begins* indicates this fact, as does his judgment that the novel is as "wretched a waste of small talent and of a reader's time as any novel published in recent years."[20]

But Princeton Keith is not in trouble because he has been so inept as to have readied for publication a manuscript not in tune with the Zeitgeist. What brings Guggelhaupt's Olympian anger down upon him is his having prepared a book that is both dirty and well-written—a ruinous combination that makes impossible its selection by either the book clubs or the Fifth Avenue bookstores for their readers. For his pains, Keith is cashiered to the Midwest, from whence he came; there, we are told, he eventually commits suicide.

That some writers are favored over others by the literary establishment we all know; again, there is also ample evidence that some authors, even after they have readied a book for publication, encounter unexpected difficulties. That publishers of highly renowned firms should engage in the shenanigans that Purdy describes should not surprise us, concerned as editors and publishers are about staying alive in a highly competitive business. At the same time, acknowledgment of the excellent writers that the Knopfs have managed to corral through the years would serve to balance Purdy's satire. Purdy's early grotesque tales were presumably presented to the Knopf firm; at the time, they may have been turned down for one reason or another. These things happen, but Purdy evidently never forgave either Knopf or his literary associates—nor did he forgive the reviewers who had been unfavorable in their reviews of his novels.

V *The Course of Love*

In *Malcolm* and in some of the earlier tales, the course of love and marriage never runs smoothly; nor does it in *Cabot*

Wright Begins, in which Purdy's treatment of both areas of experience is either hilarious or depressing. A good example of hilarious treatment is the episode in which Warburton visits Dr. Bigelow-Martin's office where the latter's Marriage-or-Death clinic is in session. Were the name of the clinic not enough to make us do a double take, the literature lying about in the doctor's waiting room quickly makes clear that the idea of living the single life in America is unthinkable, if not actually impossible, and that marriage is the "sole human" reality. The message is obvious with Warburton's glance inside the clinic; there in a quasi-religious ceremony, men, women, and children are seen on their knees intoning and promising to marry and to remain forevermore in that state of bliss.[21]

Amusing as the above episode reads, the actual marital states of the couples in the novel are sad ones; for, as in *Malcolm*, the reader is subjected to a devastating view of married life. In the case of the Cabot Wrights, all we see and know of Cabot's wife Cynthia is that she is so deeply immersed in her career as an interior designer that she has forgotten that she once promised Cabot to love, honor, and obey him. Thus, when she is finally carted off to a sanitarium, having lost her mind as a result of her husband's many sexual bouts with her, we feel little compassion because Purdy never succeeds in creating for his reader a person; instead, he presents her as an automaton devoted solely to her career.

The fiasco of the Wright marriage is only one of the four failures at mutual understanding which Purdy portrays. Another is the Warburton ménage, where husband and wife are so alienated that Warburton's first real concern about his wife Gilda comes about only after she tells him she has been raped by Cabot. Warburton, loath to believe her, thinks the rapist may have been Brady, their black butler, with whom Gilda has been very friendly. When he tells her that she smells very much like a Negress, Gilda's retort is that she should not be begrudged the "color" she finds in the few hours that she spends weekly in Harlem. Furthermore, the only reason she spends her time there is that she has too many hours alone because of Warburton's inordinate quest for wealth. When the magnate is later convinced that Cabot has indeed raped Gilda, Zenda, Goldie, and countless others, he commits suicide; but not before he has changed his will, in which Cabot's status is changed "from General Partner to God." Warburton's suicide probably denotes his final realization of the utter stupidity of his great drive for riches in a lifeless and loveless society. Contemplation of the above fact probably induced the paroxysms of laughter which had been heard by his secretary prior to Warburton's death.

The failure that epitomizes the Warburton marriage is also characteristic of the Bernie Gladhart–Carrie Moore union. Bernie, who is Carrie's fourth husband, had in fact been sent to New York by his wife, a nymphomaniac who had divorced her third husband after one look at Bernie convinced her that he had more to offer her sexually. Bernie also proves unable to satisfy Carrie's insatiable sexual desires, but not before we have been given some scenes and descriptions of their nightly sex activities in their Chicago bedroom, which Carrie has turned into a love bower. After Bernie has been sent to New York, Carrie consorts with a light-skinned Negro, Joel Ullay; and Bernie learns about their affair when he telephones Carrie about his progress in hunting for Cabot. In bed with Ullay at the time, Carrie's moans of pleasure are overheard by Bernie when she fails to hang up the receiver.

The fact that Bernie soon finds sexual solace with Zoe Bickle, who momentarily fills Carrie's place, only compounds what is already for her a loveless situation. For Zoe, bright as she is, is married to Curt Bickle, an unsuccessful novelist who deludes himself into believing in his role as a writer because his wife's salary enables him to stay at home. Here again we have the case of a writer, one so often found in Purdy's fiction, who fails to write. A Christian who does not know a word of Hebrew, Bickle spends his time annotating the book of Isaiah, an indication perhaps of how futile the whole idea of writing is. Since their marriage has lasted only because of inertia and habit, Curt and Zoe Bickle are merely tolerant of each other and in no way give each other the joy and companionship we expect of happily married people.

Amidst all this marital degradation, a sense of poignancy occurs when Bernie returns to Carrie in Chicago only to learn, as she so bluntly puts it, that "her well has gone dry." The scene

in which Bernie leaves her gazing at a television screen while
contemplating her menopause would be tragic were it not for
the fact that no sympathy can be elicited for a woman who has
given her all for sex; for not once does she say or do anything
that would reveal that she has the slightest idea of what real
love is.

If modern marriage is portrayed as a farce, the one night of
warmth and tenderness that Bernie experiences in the arms of
one Winters Hart, a married Congolese whom he meets while
out for a walk, is not. A man who walks like a prince and who
is unimpressed by anything "except what was inside him," Hart
is the "Ideal Man" for Bernie, who sees in him qualities of
character lacking in most Americans, whether white or black.
While waiting for his wife and children to join him, Hart finds
the Negroes' efforts in America to adopt the ways of white men
anything but an enviable quest. Furthermore, that he and
Bernie find solace in each other's arms for one night needs no
explanation; for, as Hart sees it, a little love here and there lifts
the burden of life for one another.[22] Thus, love is evidently
where one finds it, regardless of the sex of the couple.

VI *Weaknesses and Strengths of* Cabot Wright Begins

If a novelist intends to capture his share of readers, he is wise,
first of all, if he writes a narrative which quickly gains the reader's attention; and, in this respect, *Cabot Wright Begins* passes
the test. For from the very beginning—with the description of
Bernie Gladhart in New York looking for Cabot Wright—right
through to the end, when Cabot himself has left New York in
order to "begin"—to find out what makes him tick—the novel is
fascinating because of the many-sided attacks made on contemporary American society and life. No intelligent reader can
feel less than grateful to Purdy for having shown us our deficiencies as a people and as a nation. Yet, when we are through
with the massive indictments made about the Wall Street way
of life, the preference for money over quality which characterizes most publishing houses in their selection of books, and the
hoax that marriage is in our time, we feel that we have read
a sociological study rather than a novel; for at no time do we

really become enmeshed with the lives and problems of the main characters, the usual effect by which a novel lives and makes its impact.

This touchstone of involvement is not present to any appreciable extent in *Cabot Wright Begins*; instead, a number of people appear to have been brought together to act out certain scenes and episodes in order to flesh out certain theses. Try as we will, we find it difficult to become seriously interested in the lives of such characters as Bernie Gladhart, Zoe Bickle, Al Guggelhaupt, and Princeton Keith beyond the fact that they are all dedicated to finding Cabot and to publishing a book about his experiences. As for Cabot himself, we can follow his switch from broker to rapist, but we find it difficult to understand the reasons he advances for following this mode of conduct. An art major at college who was forced to enter Wall Street by his foster-father, Cabot seemingly lacks spiritual integrity and is not so much a person as a peg upon which to hang a double assertion: first, expressing one's will about choosing one's occupation is a rather difficult matter, and second, working in Wall Street can be the most boring job in the world. As for the first assertion, readers will view Cabot's inability to resist becoming a broker as a weakness of will, a fact that makes him less than admirable. As for the second assertion, thousands of New Yorkers who work on Wall Street will dispute the fact that their work is tedious.

Nor does the passage on personal identity at the end of the novel, when Cabot writes Zoe Bickle that he is lighting out very much like Huck Finn to find out what is real for him, add credibility or give new insight into his character. Huck had undergone the process of civilization and had seen so-called good Christian people selling souls when they sold slaves, and at least he had made his moral choice in not turning Nigger Jim over to the authorities. On the other hand, in his role of stockbroker turned rapist, Cabot Wright is seen in no such constructive light.[23] All we know is that his job bored him and that he became a rapist because he found nothing better to do. When Cabot intends to find out who he is, "since we all have personalities which somebody [Madison Avenue] had given us in the first place," it is difficult to conceive that by going off somewhere else with this kind of thinking, he will gain added insight. This knowledge would actually be available to him right where he is were he first to grow mentally. Did not Thoreau say that he had traveled much in Concord?

But of all the major male characters in Purdy's first four novels—Malcolm, Cliff, and Amos Ratcliffe in *Eustace Chisholm and The Works*—Cabot alone manages to stay alive at the end. This happy outcome is due in great measure to the efforts of Zoe Bickle, who, after having read Bernie's account of Cabot's life, sits down with Cabot to fill in those areas of his life which needed clarification; these talks with Zoe cause the former stockbroker to begin to assess the significance of his previous acts as a rapist. Made somewhat more thoughtful as a result of Zoe's ministrations, Cabot—like Warburton before him—breaks into paroxysms of laughter, an action he had not been able to engage in throughout the novel. Cabot can laugh again, and we hear him admit that laughter "is the greatest boon Nature has bestowed on miserable unjoyous man"; yet we are left wondering whether it is a happy fate for Cabot to remain alive, in light of his analysis of the human condition in which laughter merely serves as

the release, the only relief from the pain of being human, mortal, ugly, limited, in agony, watching Death cornhole you beginning with the first emergence from the winking slit above the mother's fundament, pulled into existence from between, piss and shit, sorrow and meaninglessness, drudgery and illusion, passion, pain, early loss of youth and vigor, of all that had made it worth while, with the eternity of the tomb, the final word over the hunger of God, the repletion of earth and slime, the shout of the ocean in the ears of death. Meaning is there is no meaning but the laughter of the moment made it worth while. That's all it's about.[24]

With this outlook, which evaluates life and living as nothing more than a huge Naturalistic pigsty, Cabot makes his way "to extended flight, but this time with myself. . . ." Only one other figure need concern us at this juncture, and that is Zoe Bickle, who, after helping Cabot regain his perspective, returns to Chicago, where she tells her husband that she might be tempted after all to write about Cabot's life. At the same time, she nullifies the idea by adding that she would never dare to "be a writer in a place in time like the present"; and she repudiates thus her role as a forceful character whom we can respect. For why not dare to "be a writer in a place and time like the present"? In a period of great and increasing turbulence in which our government and society have begun, however belatedly, to become more aware of the need to revise their goals and priorities, we think of the tremendous impact one book can have. *The Greening of America* by Charles Reich, for example, has caused many thoughful Americans to take serious pause to consider the whole nature and the goals of our society. So what is really needed, it would seem, of one who would "be a writer in a place and time like the present" is to present one's best ideas and, if these are dynamic enough, they will be considered and discussed by those working to improve our way of life.

If Zoe Bickle is afraid of being a writer at this time, James Purdy is not; and *Cabot Wright Begins* will remain a very important book because of Purdy's many-pronged satire of the many social, economic, and ethical ills that beset America in the 1960s. Unlike *Children Is All*, this novel received many adverse reviews. When Stanley Edgar Hyman called it "a bad, sick joke," he suggested that Purdy had missed his true vocation, that of a sick comic, for which his combination of passion and bad taste qualified him.[25] Another critic, Theodore Solotaroff, acknowledged that Purdy's satire of American values was the best thing of its kind since the work of Nathanael West; but Solotaroff still thought that Purdy had allowed his indictment to get out of hand.[26] A third reviewer, Eric Moon, who had hitherto read nothing by Purdy, found that the novel reminded him of Nabokov because of Purdy's sense of the absurd and his delight in style.[27] What seems fairly obvious by this time is that an assessment of Purdy's fiction allows for no Laodicean approach. It impresses critics and reviewers either favorably or unfavorably, but it never creates a lukewarm attitude or evaluation.

VII Eustace Chisholm and The Works

After the publication of *Cabot Wright Begins*, Purdy may have felt that his themes of loneliness, alienation, and lovelessness, which had permeated his previous fiction, were no longer valid, since the times had changed. For, by the 1960s, the more abundant life which a great many Americans had begun to experience earlier had reached a peak which belied the fact that the current mode of American life was essentially a negative and frustrating affair. As a result, in his next novel, *Eustace Chisholm and The Works*, which appeared in May, 1967, Purdy chose as his locale and period the city of Chicago during the depression years of the 1930s, the time when the United States had begun to move slowly but inexorably towards involvement in World War II.

Purdy's fourth novel was not concerned, however, with the economic lacerations that scarred so many Americans after the October, 1929, crash, nor with the great war that was soon to engulf the lives of nearly all Americans. Instead it was concerned with the theme of homosexuality, a subject that recurs throughout his fiction. An indication of the popularity of the gay life as a literary theme at this time is seen in the fact that such sordid, humorless novels as John Rechy's *City of Night* and Hubert Selby's *Last Exit to Brooklyn* enjoyed considerable success, since a great many readers were apparently avidly hungry for this kind of mental diet.

To be completely disassociated from the tawdry, dreary tone sounded by Rechy and Selby, and even from such novels as the better-written yet badly flawed *Another Country* by James Baldwin, Purdy's publishers let their readers know on the flyleaf that their author's latest opus was fundamentally about "love and the unpredictable, unexpected and almost incredible forms in which it sometimes makes an appearance in life." What this last statement really meant was that, besides homosexuality, other ingredients, such as incest and nymphomania, were also included. But, of the various "incredible forms" of love, homosexuality and its devastating effect upon the human spirit and on the lives of the afflicted are the major concerns of the novel. Because of the manner in which Purdy's hapless homosexuals meet their doom, we are reminded of the tragic fate suffered by the protagonists of Greek tragedy.

VIII   *The Anguish of Homosexuality*

Of the pathos of a specific homosexual relationship, Purdy
had written previously in *The Nephew*; in it, middle-aged Willard
Baker is shown at one point as literally begging his much
younger companion, Vernon Miller, not to leave him. In fact,
Willard offers Vernon handsome financial incentives to remain
with him and be his love. Although this poignant scene depicts
the loneliness and lack of companionship which the older man
is fearful of facing, the relationship between Willard and Vernon
does not compare in interest with the strange, and stronger,
attraction in *Eustace Chisholm* between two young men. One,
is Amos Ratcliffe, the seventeen-year-old Adonis, who is almost
too beautiful for this world; the other, a hard-bitten former
army sergeant, Daniel Haws, is a robust physical specimen who
is only a few years older than Amos. Willard Baker had been
afraid of losing the youthfulness of life which Vernon exemplified;
Daniel Haws is so psychically constituted, however, as to find
himself unable to admit that he loves another male, "that he
needed Amos, that it was Amos who dictated everything he felt
and represented all he needed."[28]

Having no money to go elsewhere, Amos has moved into an
old rooming house which Daniel owns and runs. Daniel manages
to keep his deep love and desire for the lad, who is "nearly as
soft as a girl," perfectly controlled during the day. At night,
however, his overwhelming craving for Amos transforms Daniel
into a somnambulist who is totally unaware of his nocturnal visits
to Amos's bedroom. There he cradles the boy's head against his
chest and leaves Amos completely dissatisfied with an incomplete
expression of affection. That two young men with such diverse
mentalities and backgrounds could have been attracted to each
other is an example of how "unpredictable and unexpected"
love is. Because of the Depression, each had left his own small
town in southern Illinois to make his own way in the "Windy
City." There Amos and Daniel came to know each other through
Eustace ("Ace" for short) Chisholm, whose run-down apartment
on 55th Street served as a meeting place for individuals battered
by the Depression. Ace, when we first meet him, is a down-at-
the-heels poet in his late twenties who uses newspapers on
which to write his poems. He, too, expresses homosexual ten-

dencies, and has an electric-sign painter, Clayton Harms, living with him. But this temporary affair helps fill the sexual void caused by Ace's wife, Carla, who has left him to live with another man. Despite this somewhat chaotic sexual situation, Ace still possesses a basic insight into the human psyche which enables him to see through and analyze the motives and desires of the people he befriends ("his works," as he calls these people) much better than they can themselves. Ace also has the ability to predict the future, a gift bestowed upon him by Luana Edwards, a black Spiritualist. Moreover, Ace serves as a kind of latter-day Greek chorus who furnishes background material for the reader; he also explains and interprets the actions of various of his works, the most important of whom are Amos and Daniel.

Ace's life is deeply interlaced with that of Amos Ratcliffe, and, as a result, we learn that the boy had been born out of wedlock to a woman who is referred to as Cousin Ida, with whom Amos had committed incest before he left for Chicago. Being somewhat of a child prodigy, Amos manages to obtain a University of Chicago fellowship, but when it is eventually terminated, he is too young to be eligible for relief. To keep himself mentally occupied, he teaches Attic Greek to Chisholm, who in turn gives the lad the comfort and advice he needs to carry on his daily activities. For Amos, who loves Daniel desperately, feels spurned and rejected by his landlord; as a result, his feeling of rejection makes him particularly prone to the advances of other men, both black and white, who find his handsomeness irresistible.

As for Daniel Haws, there is no question about his legitimacy. The son of a coal-miner, Daniel became one after his father died in a mine accident and left Daniel to care for his mother and the younger children. Because of his hard life, Daniel matures quickly and grows up proud of his masculinity; indeed, he regards his seduction of many girls as ample evidence of his virility. When mining coal becomes irksome, Daniel enlists in the army, where for a time his essentially hard-bitten nature finds satisfaction. Military life eventually palls, however, and Daniel, without official leave, goes to Chicago, where he manages to buy a rooming house. The lodgers who live there finally leave because they become disgruntled with the former sergeant's running his establishment much like an army barracks. At this point, Amos rents a room at Haws's place. From the first, Daniel is "unable to take his eyes off the boy's face"; yet he "could not admit that the feeling which seized him was love."[29]

Important for a better understanding of Daniel's sexual and psychological trauma is recognition of his inability to admit to an inverted passion; he simply cannot and will not bear it, for he likens it to "some physical illness at first." Prior to Amos, Daniel had been having an affair with Maureen O'Dell, a good-natured young woman whose busy life as a painter did not prevent her from becoming a nymphomaniac. Ace Chisholm, we learn, had been her first sexual mentor and advisor. When Daniel's lovemaking with Maureen leaves her pregnant, she prepares for an abortion, and the horror and gruesomeness of the operation remind us of a similar episode in Barth's *The End of the Road.*

The scene in the abortionist's operating room with its ghastly details is noteworthy for its shock-producing and nerve-numbing effect. There, the aborted son of Maureen O'Dell and Daniel Haws is literally dug out of Maureen's womb by the black abortionist, Dr. Beaufort Vance, who is no more concerned with his patient as a person than he would be with a piece of green cheese. Amos watches this harrowing scene throughout, for he is the only person Maureen could find to accompany her. The scenes picturing these two hapless and unloved persons in the abortionist's room—both spurned by Daniel Haws—and their return to Maureen's apartment following the abortion are unforgettable. A taxi refuses to stop for them because they are so forlorn in their appearance.

Daniel seeks to avoid admitting and accepting the responsibility of his love for Amos, but the message implicit throughout the novel is that Daniel must either surrender to this emotion or risk catastrophe. This inference is the only one we can draw; for when in talking to Chisholm about Amos, Daniel explains that he cannot possibly be in love with the boy, Ace's reply, "What's so special about you?," seems to suggest that since homosexual tendencies are far more prevalent than is commonly thought, Daniel need not worry about their expression in his life.

Warmed up on the subject of the intensity and the transience of love between males, Chisholm bids Daniel to "go home and take him [Amos] in your arms and tell him he's all you've got. That's what you are to him too, and you'd better hurry, for it won't last long for either of you, and so why spend any more of your time, his, or mine."[30]

Failure to comply with Ace's well-meant admonition is later the cause of Daniel's tragic death; and Daniel, in failing to be true to the other half of his bisexual nature, also establishes the circumstances that cause Amos to throw his own life away. Before Amos eventually does so, he is loved by a millionaire Reuben Masterson, a widower. Because of a previous loveless marriage, Reuben turns for solace to boys like Amos, whose face, we are told, "only comes a couple of times in a century." In Daniel's case, however, the inability to love as one aspect of his nature dictates leads him to run away from the problem by re-enlisting in the army in order to be as far removed from Amos as possible. But this escape, as we shall see, does not serve as a solution.

IX   *"Under Earth's Deepest Stream"*

Derived from Dante, "Under Earth's Deepest Stream" is Purdy's own heading for the third and final section of the novel. Interestingly enough, this was the first time he had divided any of his novels into separate sections or that he had employed symbolism to any extent in his fiction. The symbolism of the first two sections, entitled "The Sun At Noon" and "In Distortion-free Mirrors," respectively, is fairly obvious. "The Sun At Noon" would indicate the clarity, the broad-daylight openness, intensity, and inescapability of Daniel's passion for Amos. "In Distortion-free Mirrors" would signify the crystal-clear realization on Amos's part that, even after Daniel's reenlistment in the army to escape him, he would continue to love the sergeant, however much the embraces of other men, black or white, rich or poor, would tend to distract him from this purpose. Thus we are afforded a piercing insight into the hellish life a homosexual endures when his lover has gone.

"Under Earth's Deepest Stream" seemingly suggests that below the average man's apparently quiet facade, and in the subterranean regions of the mind, volcanoes of passion seethe, where desire and torment are ever ready to erupt into howling infernos, given the proper spark. In this section the one individual who erupts is Captain Stadger, a homosexual himself, and the officer under whom Daniel serves in the Southern army camp to which he was sent after his reenlistment. Daniel quickly recognizes Stadger as his nemesis, and he accordingly names him "death in circles," since the captain is the avenger of Amos's love at whose hands Daniel will suffer savage retribution. Here again is an example of the unexpected and unpredictable way that love sometimes expresses itself in our world.

In one sense Daniel can be compared to Oedipus at this point, for there is no escaping his fate as the love-driven and love-riven soldier. Just as he turned to sleepwalking when he submerged his love for Amos, he again becomes a somnambulist in the Louisiana army camp because his love for Amos cannot be submerged. Daniel's fate is sealed when Stadger is startled at the naked sergeant's entrance one night into his tent. Surprised at first, Stadger sends the sleepwalker back to his own tent and begins to search into Daniel's past record. Stadger, who has an "unappeasable ferocity or longing for this soldier's individual flesh,"[31] realizes he must first show Daniel that he knows more about him than the soldier realizes, and he stops at nothing to get Daniel's activities as a soldier completely under his control. He even has Daniel assigned directly to him for daily duty. Finally, to clinch his complete authority over the enlisted man, the captain illegally obtains some letters that Amos and Chisholm have written to Haws that reveal Amos's longing for Daniel. In one letter, Amos frankly admits that Haws is "the only one I have ever loved. Don't forget that, even if you forget me."[32]

Hell hath no fury like a woman, or perhaps a homosexual, scorned; and hell, too, is Daniel's reward, not so much for scorning Stadger's desire for him as for infuriating the captain by admitting that he still loves Amos, however much he is physically removed from him. Rather than comply with Stadger's request to renounce Amos, Daniel seals his doom by giving Stadger written permission to "do anything you want to with me . . . use me any way you now wish, sir." After this permission has been granted, "Under Earth's Deepest Stream" does indeed reveal Stadger's deeply buried yet furiously burning desire for Daniel, despite the captain's ordinarily smooth, crisp manner, one characterized in his dress by starched linen shirts and by carefully pressed shirt cuffs. But, before Stadger can begin to enjoy Daniel's body, he must first drive Amos's image from Daniel's mind. Doing so is no mean feat because Daniel becomes increasingly and agonizingly aware, through Chisholm's letters, of Amos's rapid moral and physical degeneration. Realizing his responsibility for this decline and fall of the boy's character, Haws is literally ready to die because he withheld his love from the boy.

Having his deepest sexual instincts denied has deeply adverse effects on Stadger's character, and it literally drives him insane. If enjoying Daniel's body means cutting out a previous portion of the sergeant's life with Amos, Stadger is prepared to do just that; for, if Daniel will not willingly become his lover, the sergeant will not live to become anyone else's love, determined as Stadger is to castrate him. Thus Stadger works out many carefully staged scenes to have Daniel willingly surrender to him; meeting only with rebuffs, Stadger ties a willing Daniel to a tree in a scene of unparalleled cataclysmic ferocity. With thunder and lightning underscoring the action, Stadger's madness completely takes over. Using some Medieval instrument of torture, he "began his work, pushing like flame . . . into Daniel's groin upward and over," thus totally emasculating the recalcitrant soldier.

Knowing all the while that death in some form awaited him at the hands of Stadger, Daniel attempted several times to escape his fate, but in each instance circumstances worked against him. Moving slowly and relentlessly toward his fate, much like Oedipus compelled by the fierce desire to know the circumstances of his birth, Haws allows his options to escape vengeance to become fewer and fewer until he is cornered and lashed to a tree by Stadger. That the officer commits suicide after disemboweling Daniel only completes the horrible cycle of what sometimes happens when love makes its unpredictable appearance in this world and is scorned.

In the fusion of theme, in character portrayal, and in setting and tone, "Under Earth's Deepest Stream" contains some of

Purdy's finest writing; and while some may quibble about the Gothic and melodramatic sense of horror that surrounds Daniel's disembowelment, the sheer power of the writing makes the scene credible.

X *Without God in the World*

Horrible and anguished as the condition of homosexuality is, and has so far been portrayed, Daniel indicates, in writing to Ace from camp of Stadger's ominous designs upon him, the one way that he might have escaped his ultimate fate. Admitting his still unremitting love for Amos, Daniel states, "If there was God for me, I would be on my knees all day, all night, I would have entered a religious order, but there is no-nothing for me but Amos, and now the army—I need it, and the army I can see sees I need it."[33]

In his failure to look beyond the material senses and in concluding that there is no God for him, Daniel portrays his spiritual bankruptcy. Moreover, his statement lacks conviction, since he is never for a moment shown really struggling to find out whether "there [is] a God for me." Interestingly enough, one religion that might rid Daniel of his plaint that "there is no-nothing for me but Amos," namely, Christian Science, Purdy holds up to ridicule as he had previously done in *The Nephew.*

The precarious nature of homosexual love in modern life is best illustrated by the dust jacket of the novel, illustrating a small but beautifully shaped moth heading towards the palm of a man's hand. The moth might possibly symbolize the brittle and tenuous sense of love which homosexuality is at best, despite its intensity in the case of Amos and Daniel. The hand might denote the manner in which this love moth is received; in Stadger's case, this love would be completely crushed, overwhelmingly obsessed as he is with Haws. In any event, the final impression we gain is a tremendous sense of compassion for the hopeless nature of homosexual love in a world without God.

XI *Weaknesses and Strengths of*
Eustace Chisholm and The Works

Granted the strength and craftsmanship expended in portraying the hellish and frustrating life that homosexuality in-

volves, the novel—despite the excellent writing to be found in
"Under Earth's Deepest Stream"—is open to criticism on at
least two accounts: it lacks certain aspects of credibility about
various circumstances, and, far more important, the major
characters lack significance and verisimilitude.

First, certain aspects of credibility try the reader's patience.
For example, when Haws is washing his mess kit after a meal,
he sees lying on the ground before him a newspaper with a
picture of Amos uppermost, telling of the latter's death. Mis-
taken as a housebreaker, Amos had been shot to death by a
Chicago policeman. It is understandable, of course, that Daniel
must be apprised of Amos's death, for now he can no longer
make reparations to the one he had never told his love. As a
result, Haws is psychologically ready to be emasculated by
Stadger, since he has nothing for which to live. Nonetheless,
the incident of Amos' photograph in the newspaper seems a
bit farfetched, since photographs of purported housebreakers
are usually not considered sufficiently important to be printed
in newspapers.

Credibility is also strained in the epilogue of the novel where
Ace Chisholm, when lighting a match to search for some material,
manages to ignite a large batch of newspapers on which he had
written his poems. We again have an example of the typical
Purdian writer who, in some way or another, manages to be
unsuccessful—in this case, because of the fire. The one newspaper that is salvaged contains a long column of print with
pictures of the marriage of Reuben Masterson and Maureen
O'Dell. As previously noted, Masterson had been one of Amos's
lovers after Haws had reenlisted; and Maureen was the young
painter who had undergone an abortion. The fire, happening
as it does, is perhaps a good device to tie up the loose ends of
the plot; but its use seems woefully Hardyesque in context.
The unlikeliest action, however, is the scene in which Daniel,
completely disemboweled, is shown staggering back to camp,
"carrying his bowels in his hands like provisions" and screaming
"Kill me, for I've stood all tests and you owe me my death."[34]
To picture a man who has been emasculated as not dying almost
immediately because of loss of blood and the shock sustained
but as strong enough to get back to camp on his own, is, to say

the least, extraordinary; and the mind certainly boggles at the thought that he can speak coherently enough to request that he be killed.

Aside from these examples of incredibility, we have the larger question of the verisimilitude of the characters themselves. Publicity in the last few years has thrown much light on homosexuality and on the attendant circumstances and conditions from which it evolves. And, while thoughtful citizens may become more understanding and more aware of this sexual phenomenon, we query whether a novel almost totally involved with this subject is not inflating an aspect of human existence that is at best only an abnormal sexual experience. Sophocles bade us see life steadily and to see it whole, but the homosexual love in Purdy's latest opus seems to be the be-all and end-all of human existence. So distorted are the sexual relationships in the novel that never once is a normal love affair between a man and a woman portrayed, as it might have been, to serve as a contrast. Even the heterosexual relationship of Reuben Masterson and Maureen O'Dell is a farce, since he is a homosexual, and she is a nymphomaniac. In Masterson's case, there is the hilarious yet grim irony that, in having married Maureen, there will be no real happiness between the two; for Masterson sees himself as going to bed with the boys whom Maureen will bring home to sate her own physical desires.

When we are told, therefore, that the theme of the novel is love and the "unpredictable, unexpected forms in which it sometimes makes an appearance in life," we wonder whether it is not lust and the strong sexual desire attendant upon it that is meant. Were it really love, there would be some sense of caring on the part of the various individuals for each other which love connotes; but very little feeling of this type exists in the novel.

The figure most lacking credibility is Ace Chisholm, who is so involved with himself that his character borders on egotism. As a modern Greek chorus, commenting on past and present actions, his role seems somewhat unrealistic. He gives sexual advice in a manner that shows he really does not care for the people he advises. He tells Maureen O'Dell, whom he was the first to seduce, to have as many sexual affairs as possible in order to tear away the foundations of her religious faith. In so doing, he reveals himself as a somewhat benighted character and as the antithesis of the ancient Greek choruses, whose utterances nearly always spoke of the need for restraint and responsibility for one's actions.

Thus, the one-dimensional role of his character makes him a highly unlikely person to know better than themselves the people, "the works," who congregate around him. Were Ace's somewhat shallow view of life not enough to make him highly suspect for the position he fills, we also have the problem created by his mantle of clairvoyance, which is bestowed upon him by Luana Edwards, a Negress fortune-teller. This gift enables him to divine what is eventually going to befall Daniel Haws at the hands of Stadger; but, when Ace foresees the tragedy that envelopes Haws, our own judgment and life experience causes us to question Ace's capability for such perception. Had he impressed us as one who had the mentality of an Isaiah or a Jeremiah, we might believe in him; otherwise, we cannot.

Still Ace foresees Haws's death at Stadger's hands. And, as if to signify that lack of creativity or death is the fate of those who engage in homosexuality, Ace is shown at the end of the novel as giving up his writing of poetry and as returning to a hetero-sexual love when he is seen possessing his wife Carla "with a kind of ravening love." If heterosexual love is intended to denote the cessation of creative activity, in this case the writing of poetry, we are left in a quandary as to what kind of love stimu-lates artistic creation. Do homosexuals write better than hetero-sexuals? If so, how do we account for writers such as Hawthorne, Howells, and Twain, among others, who wrote their best works after marriage? Whether heterosexuals are better writers than homosexuals we do not know; but we do know that, in Purdy's fiction, artists and writers, all of whom are married, do not fare well. For, besides Ace, we are reminded of Kermit Raphaelson and Eloisa Brace, the two painters in *Malcolm;* Parkhearst Cratty in *63: Dream Palace;* and the two Bickles in *Cabot Wright Begins.* All of these characters are depicted as never producing a true work of art.

Despite the many disparate kinds of "love" and the cheer-lessness that pervades it, the strength of *Eustace Chisholm and*

The Works lies in its creation of a homosexual world in which these people live, have their being, but do not always possess the bodies of those they love. At times, certain episodes may seem repellent to the average reader, whose experience of love may be far removed from the type depicted here. Nonetheless, these episodes serve a worthwhile purpose in that they may help us understand the plight and anguish of homosexuals. In Purdy's treatment of these unfortunate individuals, he evokes a tremendous sense of pity; and he simultaneously portrays the nihilism and power of blackness which pervade the experience of the gay people. Written carefully, even hauntingly beautiful at times, *Eustace Chisholm and The Works* should endure as an able, compassionate treatment in fiction of one of modern society's more urgent problems.

XII   *The Critics Once Again*

As with Purdy's previous works of fiction, *Eustace Chisholm and The Works* enjoyed the same diversity of critical views, but some reviewers deemed the novel highly satisfactory. Among these early yea-sayers were Wilfrid Sheed and Angus Wilson; and Sheed, noting that the book had overall interest "only if . . . viewed as a work of black nihilism," thought that Purdy was saying exactly what was on his mind in the scenes he had created and that, in so doing, he had written his best prose so far.[35] Wilson regarded the work as "a remarkable achievement," and he called Purdy a master when it came to the "mixing of the horrible, the wildly funny and the very sad."[36]

Other critics who were positive in their reactions included Irving Malin, Ross Wetzsteon, and Richard K. Morris. Malin regarded the story as primarily a study of "perversity" and as an attempt on Purdy's part to reach out for universal truths. While the novel violated our civilized sensibilities, more important was the fact that it gave the reader the "painful pleasure of recognizing the incredible nature of love."[37] Ross Wetzsteon made no bones about his admiration for the work, which he regarded as Purdy's finest novel.[38] Tracing the various themes in previous Purdy fiction, all of which seemed to be a search for the proper expression of love, as in the "ravening love" Ace

finally bestowed on his wife, Wetzsteon found for the first time
an authentic note of love, hope, and compassion in Purdy's
fiction. According to Morris, Purdy in his latest novel was seeking a love that was basically pure and simple; but, given the
nature of life, this search became a hard and frustrating one;
still, the search was the one thing in the world that mattered.
And, while the novel could be described as a homosexual one,
it was not so in the sense that the novels of John Rechy and
William Burroughs were; instead, Purdy was endeavoring to
describe the aberration, the isolation, and lovelessness that the
gay life entailed.[39]

Some of the critics who disagreed with such affirmative assess-
ments included Barry Gross and Warren Coffey. Gross found the
novel disappointing, since the very qualities for which Purdy
was noted—sharp contrast, jolting ironies, and colliding contradictions—were missing.[40] Even more disappointing was the fact
that each time he looked forward, as he felt others did, to a new
novel by Purdy for something commensurate with "our capacity
for wonder," he was disappointed. In *Malcolm,* he found the
bizarre; in *The Nephew,* the banal. However, in *Cabot Wright
Begins* and *Eustace Chisholm and The Works,* both the bizarre
and the banal were present; but, alas, no wonder was to be
found.

Even more negative was the review by Warren Coffey. While
admitting Purdy's great talent in the area of the Gothic and
surrealistic, especially when the plot dealt with people whose
specialness was of a sexual nature, Coffey found Purdy's latest
novel far from satisfactory.[41] He thought the last section, where
Stadger and Haws have their final confrontation, to be interesting and well-written, but he asserted that the work was really
a *novella* that was dragged out to the length of a novel. Moreover, in Purdy's treatment of Maureen O'Dell and her raison
d'être, Coffey found the author's portrayal of the woman altogether inept and snide. To account for Purdy's faults in handling
several of his characters and the structure of the novel, Coffey
found a great sense of petulance in the author's attitude toward
life. As far as Coffey was concerned, Purdy had never forgiven
his boyhood, the Ohio towns he lived in, the Depression years,
and many of the dark and terrible wounds he doubtless had

received as a youngster. As a result, nearly all of his books had come to "resemble a wheelchair careening in ever narrowing circles," always returning to the theme of the lost childhood. In *Cabot Wright Begins*, Purdy had momentarily broken this circle with a satire of American institutions; and his petulance had become ridicule. But in *Eustace Chisholm and The Works*, Purdy had returned to his old theme of lost children. Accordingly, the inability to grow beyond this repetitive theme had kept Purdy from introducing a larger range of characters and a larger view of the real world; as a result, his lost children can never be seen in their proper relation to reality. Unless Purdy could succeed in resolving his own sense of petulant deprivation, Coffey "bet against his ever writing a genuine novel."

CHAPTER 6

The Novel as Nostalgia: Jeremy's Version

ON October 11, 1970, a full-page advertisement about Purdy's latest novel appeared in the *New York Times Book Review*, and the caption read: "American fiction is alive and well. In fact, James Purdy has never been better."[1] Made by Doubleday & Company, Purdy's current publisher, this thought-provoking and resounding statement would be amusing at best and arrogant at worst in its equating the whole range and welfare of modern American fiction with a single writer—and particularly with one whose fiction has never received the consistently complimentary reviews of such contemporaries as Bellow, Malamud, Updike, and Mailer, to mention just a few. Yet in making the above pronouncement, Doubleday was certainly signifying that in *Jeremy's Version* Purdy had a winner, one which could establish him beside other authors in the Doubleday fold such as Kate Millett, Taylor Caldwell, and Jean Kerr whose current books—*Sexual Politics, Great Lion of God,* and *Penny Candy*—were then best sellers from coast to coast.

Although Purdy's works will in all probability never make the best-seller lists, for reasons already discussed, we can understand Doubleday's enthusiasm for *Jeremy's Version.* A regional novel of the Midwest—a genre particularly felicitous to Purdy and one which he had previously assayed successfully in *The Nephew* —*Jeremy's Version* is a fascinating novel which evokes nostalgia for the 1920s. With his keen ear and eye for the nuances of small-town life and speech, as well as his use of such place names as Devil's Spire, Frog Hollow, Paulding Meadows, and Ojibway Creek, which literally reek with atmosphere, Purdy educes the tang and flavor of the Midwest at an earlier time in this century. Set somewhere in a "Yankee State," probably Ohio, the novel is highly satisfactory for two reasons: it not only exudes the small-town atmosphere of the years President Warren G. Harding

109

and President Calvin Coolidge were in the White House, but it also transcends its immediate surroundings by virtue of the universality of its theme and characters.

According to Doubleday, *Jeremy's Version* is the first work of a trilogy, collectively entitled *Sleepers in Moon-Crowned Valleys*, which will be concerned with the people and towns of America's Midwest. This continuity of subject marks a departure for Purdy, whose novels hitherto have been diversified thematically; however, by adhering geographically for some time to the Midwest, Purdy evidently means to mine the literary ore in which the region abounds; and his doing so will mean great riches for future American fiction if *Jeremy's Version* is an indication of what may be expected. Noteworthy depicters of the Midwest have been few and far between since Edgar Lee Masters, Sherwood Anderson, and Sinclair Lewis, all of whom made their major impact in the 1920s. Giving added interest to middle America at present is the fact that it is regarded as the region where the values and mores which have made America great in the past apparently still abide, if we properly assess the great importance attached to this area by the Nixon administration.

Whatever the reasons Purdy has elected to concentrate on middle America, he is an excellent regionalist; for *Jeremy's Version* is his best novel to date. Fascinating to read, the novel reveals Purdy's talents as a storyteller at their peak.

I *From Time Immemorial*

In returning to the terrain he had portrayed in *The Nephew*, Purdy has delineated at some length for the first time an entire American family—parents, children, and relatives. The manner in which their hopes, aspirations, and lives impinge upon one another in nearly every case results in frustration for all of them. The narrative is concerned with a situation which in origin and theme can be traced to the tales of antiquity: a mother is left to rear her children because the father has deserted them. Elvira Fergus, comely and thirtyish, has the onerous task of rearing her three sons—Rick, Jethro, and Rory—while simultaneously serving as the mistress-owner of a boardinghouse, the economic base for her family. She is in this predicament because Wilders Fergus, her husband and the father of the boys, has been a ne'er-do-well from almost the beginning of their marriage, in 1908; and his flights from his family are portrayed as recurring acts right through the 1920s.

An up-and-coming young banker when he decided to marry the exceedingly pretty sixteen-year-old choir singer Elvira Summerlad, the tall and handsome Wilders Fergus had only one goal in life: to become extremely wealthy so as to care for his family in good style. As we might expect, he never attains his objective; but, to compound his failure, he ruins many people financially, including members of his wife's family, as well as other relatives. In fact, bankruptcy is all that Wilders has to offer Elvira shortly after their marriage. As a result, the woman's life becomes one of fending off creditors seeking payment while Wilders seeks somewhere the golden fleece which constantly eludes him. Tired of their penurious life in Hattisleigh, where the couple had married, the family moves to Boutflour, "a gingerbready county seat of a town," where Elvira's troubles start in earnest. Previously, Wilders had been of some help to her; but now he leaves her to fend for herself while he remains away for long periods of time in his aimless quest for wealth. Becoming the owner of a thirty-room house, which has been deeded to her by an old friend, Elvira works very hard to barely make ends meet. Simultaneously, she tyrannizes her boys during their father's absence from home, and they easily succumb to her domineering ways.

When Wilders decides to return to Boutflour after a particularly long absence, his return is aided and abetted by his spinster sister Winifred, who had hated Elivira from the beginning, and who had attempted to prevent her marriage to Wilders. Elvira, her good looks having begun to fade because of her travail, has finally decided to divorce her long-estranged husband. As might be expected in a small town of the 1920s, the idea of divorce is repugnant to both Winifred and Wilders because of their Presbyterian upbringing; and their opposition to the destruction of the marriage gives the novel its dominant thrust. That Elvira ultimately obtains her divorce (but with results she had not previously anticipated) is almost anticlimactic because of other actions and incidents that take place between her initial suit and the eventual decree.

Significantly, Elvira is not the major character in the novel, for the dominant figure is her second son, the fourteen-year-old Jethro, who, having suffered a nearly fatal head injury at the age of six, had fully recovered. However, in the process, he had irreparable damage done to his psyche and had gained deep insights into the evils of life. These evils and his reflections upon them, which he recorded in a notebook, were based upon the activities that occurred both in and outside the boarding-house. His "log," which later falls into the hands of various people, quickly notes that his mother is a whore because he has seen her from time to time enter the little cottage in back of the boardinghouse with some of its male members. At the same time, theatrically-minded brother Rick, aged twenty, has also incurred Jethro's hatred. For Rick, Boutflour has become a veritable Gehenna from which he wishes to escape as quickly as possible in order to become an actor. Out of frustration at having to remain in town longer than he wished, Rick has begun to torment Jethro from time to time. Having managed somehow to get his hands on letters sent to Rick by both his male and female admirers, Jethro is confirmed in his belief that life is essentially evil; for the letters reveal that Rick has given his body to anyone who would promote his thespian career.

The reader who has kept a close watch over Jethro's mental processes is not surprised when the youngster attempts to shoot his mother during the fairgrounds supper that Elvira holds for her family and friends after her divorce has been granted. He deeply loves her, but she has given her body to various men.

However, his attempt at murder is nullified by Matt Lacey, an ardent admirer of Elvira's, who, though only a year older than Rick, has become his friend and advisor. With Agnes Cole—the handsome strawberry-blonde piano teacher who is Elvira's un-married friend—and the typical gossips to be found in small towns, the cast of characters for our understanding of Purdy's intent in *Jeremy's Version* is fairly complete.

II *Technical Devices*

Jeremy's Version is by far the most intricately structured of Purdy's novels. Although the tale of the Sumerlad and Fergus families is told by Matt Lacey, the narration actually takes place many years after the events narrated; Matt is now an old man, and all of the major characters are deceased. What takes place is, therefore, a tale within a tale; for Matt has managed to hire a latter-day prototype of Jethro Fergus, one Jeremy Cready, also a fourteen-year-old, to serve as his amanuensis. But, where Jethro Fergus regarded life with a baleful eye, Jeremy is more a modern version of Huck Finn; and, like Twain's youngster, he is much wiser than his fourteen years would imply.

Aiding and abetting Matt as a raconteur is the fact that, along with his deep love for the people whom he has come to know and cherish during his lifetime, he has learned the essential facts of both families through Jethro's damning journal, from the letters written Rick by his admirers, and from other pertinent materials. Although he is in an excellent position to be the narrator, he is fortunate that young Jeremy Cready comes along at the right time—first as a newspaper boy and later as a notetaker when he is expelled from school for poor work and simultaneously loses his newspaper delivery job. Matt enables his young charge to become more fully aware of the two families who form "the story that was the master passion of his life" by having the boy take home a sheaf of papers dealing with the Summerlads and the Ferguses. Thus Jeremy gains his own "version" of the characters and their lives; and his doing so provides the title of the novel. Della Gasman, Jeremy's half sister, knows, like Matt, all of the people involved, but she has disparate views about certain aspects of Matt's recital; her views tend to round out the narrative for Jeremy, who had never known the Ferguses and the Summerlads.

As a result what might at first seem an intricate and involved narrative pattern is only Matt's account of the contents of Jethro's journal which Jeremy takes down in long hand. This narrative design affords no chapter divisions as such; instead incidents, episodes, character descriptions, and reminiscences are recounted in long or short passages, as befits their significance in Matt's eyes. A sense of verisimilitude derives from Matt's having Jeremy take down things that come to him at any moment from out of the past. As a result, variety and change of tone are gained in the reminiscences, which otherwise might have become monotonous had they been told in straightforward chronological sequence.

How deeply Matt Lacey cherishes all of the characters whose lives he draws from his well of memories and recollections is seen in his use of ventriloquism to imitate their speech and voice mannerisms, for so vividly does he remember their personalities. Yet while he relates his chronicle, which runs on interminably, there are pauses after two incidents which end in rape, thus giving both Jeremy and Matt an opportunity to leave the past and return to present-day reality. That the characters Matt conjures up from the past are no longer alive does not in any way lessen the interest of his recital for the reader; for Matt, who had been an actor in his adult life, makes these dead people come forcefully to life; and this capability makes the novel fascinating reading.

III *The Heart Has Reasons*

Revolving around Elvira, her efforts to rear her children, and finally her intent to rid herself of a derelict husband, the novel is most successful in presenting the major characters and their different modes of reasoning, particularly Elvira's. Only sixteen when she met her future husband, she was swept off her feet. But Elvira has legitimate reasons for acting in the manner she later does. For, from the beginning, her marriage was literally under the "curse" of her sister-in-law Winifred's meddling. Winifred's attempt to break up her brother's marriage had even included an unsuccessful trip to Elvira's home expressly for that purpose. Winifred's continued animosity toward her, together with Wilders's leaving her in "a family way" each time he returns and with nothing more, are matters for which Elvira no longer can forgive her husband. Yet what most infuriates Elvira about Wilders after twenty years of marriage is "that he knew certainly so little of human motives, for he didn't know men and hadn't a ghost of a notion what a woman was," except as a sex object.[2] Understandable if not altogether moral then, are her occasional sexual adventures with her boardinghouse guests, since, for all practical purposes, she does not have a husband to satisfy her sensual nature.

Elvira is also insatiable in her desire to control the lives of her boys, for whom she feels she has sacrificed so much; and such is her physical magnetism that she ensnares older men, as well as youngsters like Matt Lacey, whom she treats as a "fourth son." A Midwesterner who can trace her roots to ancestors who fought in the Revolutionary War, Elvira is a "queen dethroned," as Della Gasman remembers her. If her sexual soirees indicate her immorality, Elvira still manages to carry on as a capable proprietress of her boardinghouse. She is respected by all her guests, if not wholeheartedly by Rick and Jethro, both of whom wish to escape her domineering ways. All told, Elvira is a woman whose life since her early marriage has not only been hard, but made much more difficult than she had reason to expect it to be; thus the reader can in a degree understand the motives behind her actions even if he does not always agree with them.

Wilders's motives for acting as he does are also understandable. The youngest, as well as the handsomest, in a family whose Scottish ancestry could be traced to the Battle of Culloden, Wilders was the most spoiled of the five Fergus children—four sons and the daughter Winifred. Wilders's being spoiled explains perhaps his inability to have a sense of responsibility towards his wife and sons; for, as his sister so succinctly states, "instead of buckling down and getting a steady job with a steady income you're always in search of some soapbubble get-rich scheme, and the rest of us . . . have had to bear the burden of your imprudence and folly, of your very expensive continuous daydreams, chasing after the rainbow in other people's lives and investments. . . ."[3]

Wilders neither smokes nor drinks, but his philandering and ruining people financially outweigh any good qualities he may possess. Moreover, he has still not learned after some twenty years to stop exploiting people in his get-rich-quick schemes. He even enlists Elvira's aid in "borrowing" six thousand dollars that Rick had recently received as an inheritance—money which the young man meant to use to get away from home and to start his stage career. "Twould help all of us towards a better future" is Wilders's remark at this point.

Elvira's motives too at this point are not altogether honest, for Rick without his inheritance will be forced to remain in Boutflour, something she deeply desires. Wilders's craving for his son's inheritance betrays a lack of moral scruples and a basic callousness which are too gross to excuse; and to his sense of impracticality and improvidence can be added his lack of sexual restraint:

his rape of Agnes Cole, to whom he has imputed Elvira's desire for a divorce. Agnes smokes; and since "a woman who smoked in that remote epoch [the 1920's] would do anything," Wilders's passion to possess her is ignited when he goes to see her, ostensibly to find out whether there might not be a chance to patch things up with Elvira. Anything Agnes might have done to restrain Wilders would have been futile; for, as Wilders sees his situation, "he had suffered too many humiliations in the past days, years. . . ."[4]

The best insight into Wilders's motives may be found in his reflections about what he had found written about himself in his son Jethro's journal. The boy had noted that his father was a womanizer and a mishandler of other people's money. "A long career behind him of being a ladies' man, he repeated, to himself. Well, he said, why not? why shouldn't it be again?"[5] Although the rape of Agnes Cole is foreordained when he goes to see her, Wilders is not really an evil man but an immoral one, whose thoughtlessness and superficiality are his dominant traits of character. Yet with his two younger boys, Jethro and Rory, he is a huge success because they long for their father, a role he has really not filled for them.

Wilders's one manly action is to contest the divorce suit, but even in this instance his hand is forced by his sister Winifred, who tells him, "I'll handle Elvira, Wilders, you can rest assured on that score,"[6] a remark appropos of her desire to stop the suit, which is against her religious upbringing. Unlike any of her four brothers, all of whom are handsome, Winifred is plain-looking; but she is not the typical old maid we would expect in a family where all of the boys had been lavished with love and where she had been taken for granted. Forceful and strong as a warrior (Elvira indicates she would have made a good first sergeant), Winifred had never interested herself in men, having been engrossed from childhood on in the lives of her brothers.

This deep involvement can best be seen in her having successfully broken up the intended marriage of her oldest brother Garret; this success made her think she could do likewise in regard to Wilders and Elvira. Having been a schoolteacher in Boston during her younger years, Winifred had never married. Thus when Elvira starts her divorce suit, Winifred is literally driven out of her mind by jealousy, for she is consumed by "Elvira's embodiment and epitome of sex and womanhood, and more terribly yet, motherhood, and her own cankering sterile virginity."[7] However simplistic Wilders's observation that his sister was merely a busybody who minded everybody's business but her own might seem to be, there may be some validity to it in light of Winifred's lack of sexual fulfillment. In one dramatic confrontation with Elvira, who is angered by Winifred's accusations about being a poor mother to her boys, Elvira tears Winifred's dress off her back. Wearing only her drawers, the spinster merely walks out of the house to a gas station half a block away; there she telephones Rick to bring her his topcoat, an action indicative of the "sergeant's" ability to maintain her sangfroid.

Never having been ill a day in her life, Winifred becomes excruciatingly sick after she reads Jethro's journal, which the boy had inadvertently left lying about. Revolted by its contents, Winifred's illness is actually psychosomatic; for her mind has been temporarily overcome by the filth in her nephew's revelations of human nature. All in all, Winifred is not a mere busybody; and her aversion to a divorce and what it would mean to her nephews to legally lose their father is understandable in light of her Presbyterian upbringing. Also understandable is Winifred's desire to remove her nephews from their mother's care because of Elvira's immoral sexual activities and because of the swilling of liquor by the male inhabitants of the boardinghouse, for both are activities that Winifred views as entirely inappropriate to the right climate for rearing a family.

Altogether different in temperament from Winifred Fergus is Agnes Cole. After a brief fling as a song writer in New York, where she had given birth to an illegitimate child, Agnes gave the child away for adoption. A very handsome woman, who greatly resembles Elvira in looks, Agnes has returned to Boutflour, seemingly to spend the rest of her days teaching piano to the children of the rich families in town. Quiet and self-contained, she manages to live without scandal; and, as Rick's piano teacher, she gets to know Elvira and Wilders well. All told, Agnes is seemingly the last person in the world to incite rape, although her brief sexual fling in New York is still remembered by some of the town's gossips.

As friends, Agnes and Elvira relate to each other their daily activities and irritations; but, when really private matters come up, both women remain silent. Agnes by her calm manner has led many troubled men and women in town to consider her to be the one person they would make their confidante. Regarded as a circumspect person who is told "everything" by these people, we find that Agnes, in turn, recounts her delicious tidbits of information to other people supposedly as trustworthy as herself. The result is that Agnes's "secrets were carefully kept until everybody knew them and could gossip about them openly."[8]

IV Like Mother, Like Son(s)

Elvira worships her son Rick, but at the same time she dominates his life. The oldest of the three boys, Rick is exceedingly handsome, possesses theatrical talent, and is the one person who can support his mother in her suit against his father, for whom Rick has become a substitute in an almost incestuous sense. Rick's desire to leave home is tempered by his realization that to be a success there or anywhere in America, "one had to be common in every fiber of his being."[9] This view, of course, is in line with Purdy's indictment of the shoddiness of much in American life. Such is Elvira's forcefulness, however, that he promises to stay until she obtains her divorce. A clerk in the office of the chief oil company in town, Rick spends most of his spare time with failed artists and members of the local intelligentsia who gather at Dr. Gray's home, where, according to town gossips, depraved actions occur.

Rick's best and most dramatic moment comes in court; for, reluctant to defame his father and opposed to the divorce, he gives testimony only after his friend Matt informs him that he has to take a stand one way or another for one of his parents. Realizing that he will be playing a far greater dramatic role in court than anything he will play on stage, he questions his father directly, posing this urgent request: "Give me ... Wilders, the reason for my existence, since you were never here before to teach it to me, and I had only Elvira to crush out manhood with her lessons."[10] This outburst in the courtroom serves only to denigrate Elvira's character in the eyes of the townspeople and to impede the quest for her decree. Sometime later—after

Rick, Jethro, and Rory have written letters that testify to Wilders's unworthiness as a father to the presiding judge—the judge does grant a decree.

Rick was born in the sunlight of her hometown, Hattisleigh, as Elvira puts it; but Jethro first saw daylight in a sunless hour in Boutflour. As if to accompany the lack of physical light at the boy's entrance into the world, there is a lack of psychic warmth in his spiritual makeup—a deficiency resulting from the nearly mortal head wound he had suffered as a youngster. Looked after tenderly by his mother during his convalescence, Jethro develops an Oedipus complex which is in direct contrast to Elvira's latent incestuous feelings for Rick. Additionally complicating the boy's feelings is the realization that Elvira does not love him as much as she does Rick. Alienated by these two wounds to his head and heart, Jethro—much like Jeremy, who will later write of him—gains his knowledge of the seamy side of life not only from his reading of French and Continental novels, but also from his observations of the actions of those around him. As a result, the notes in his log record the sins committed by those dearest and nearest him. No wonder then that Wilders, who accidentally manages to pick up the journal, believes Jethro must be "touched" when he starts reading its contents. His sister Winifred's reaction, however, is to the contrary; she realizes that these outpourings are only too true.

The sins that Jethro records may be construed as fiction by some who peruse his journal, but the boy learns sadly from his own life experience that the evil around him is only too true. For love, which he had "supposed to smell of April and May" was soon to reek with "a slaughterhouse stench." For in one episode, Vicki, the attractive young girl who helps Elvira around the house, bids him to make love to her. Vicki had previously been raped by one of the boarders, Garner, who had been "soft" about the girl ever since he had first become a lodger. Only when Garner relates to Jethro his rape of Vicki does the boy first understand and begin "to feel as Aunt Winifred and Wilders must have felt as they leafed through his notebooks." But, with Garner's crestfallen recital of the rape, Jethro realizes that "it was not this time his own kind of terrible thing, which familiarity and close knowledge had robbed of some of its sting, but somebody else's terror and shame."[11] If we consider that the boy was seduced by Vicki, who felt she owed Jethro this experience, we can better understand the boy's complete revulsion to life and to the sordid aspects of sex. The love he desires of his mother is a foul love he cannot accept, and the sexual experience he has had with Vicki reeks of the same stench.

When Elvira later hints at her boy's peculiar behavior to others, Matt becomes increasingly aware of Jethro's strange and erratic actions. It is he who saves Elvira's life at the fairgrounds supper; for, increasingly demented by his ambivalent attitude toward his mother, Jethro shoots at her, only to have Matt lunge awkwardly, receive the bullet himself, and sustain a slight wound. To explain his matricidal action, Jethro makes this admission to Matt: "Maybe I have seen about everything ... and on account of all I've seen I can imagine what the rest's like too, can't I?"[12]

Purdy has been a careful craftsman from the outset of his career, but in no previous novel has he so thoughtfully worked out the problems, motivations, and aspirations of his characters as in *Jeremy's Version*. Seen in proper perspective, the novel is a perfect mosaic of thought and action that embraces the Gallic dictum that, in order to forgive all, we must first understand all.

V Similarities of Jeremy's Version to Previous Works

After completing *Jeremy's Version*, the first work of *Sleepers in Moon-Crowned Valleys*—Purdy's projected trilogy of the Midwest in the twentieth century—we ardently hope that Purdy's writing in the future will take a different direction from that of prior novels. For, in reading the novel carefully and in noting that two entire families serve as the main characters instead of the usual orphans who dominate his fiction, we can begin to appreciate the criticism given by Warren Coffey to an earlier Purdy novel, *Eustace Chisholm and The Works*. Coffey's review noted that Purdy had been so deeply hurt by early childhood experiences that he repeats throughout his fiction themes, incidents, and attitudes related to his wounds. If this pattern of writing continues, Coffey feels that Purdy will never be able to write a genuine novel.

We are not surprised, therefore, when orphans once again play a large part in *Jeremy's Version*. One orphan, Matt Lacey, we are told, moves from Elvira's boardinghouse after she files her divorce suit only because, having lost his father, he cannot bear the thought that Rick, his closest friend, will bear witness against Rick's own father Wilders. Too, for all the good Wilders has done for them when away from home, the condition of orphanhood can be applied to his three sons. Thus, once more we have the quest for a father that is one of the themes in *Malcolm*. Moreover, in the case of Jeremy, the notetaker, we encounter the same resiliency of spirit, that hardihood of character that epitomized Amos Ratcliffe and Daniel Haws after they had to depend on themselves during the Depression years in *Eustace Chisholm and The Works.*

As for loveless fathers and mothers who to a great degree cause the unhappiness of their children, Elvira and Wilders Fergus recall the domineering mother and futile father previously encountered in such stories as "Why Can't They Tell You Why?" and "Color of Darkness." Furthermore, in Jethro's desire to kill his mother, whom he deeply loves, we are reminded of Fenton Riddleway's killing of his brother Claire. In so doing Fenton believed he would be uniting his younger brother with their mother, whom Claire had so deeply loved before she died. Nor should we forget that Jethro's morbid character is very similar to Claire's at the time Fenton kills him.

Rape, is, of course, one of the outlets for Purdy's characters when their desire for love is thwarted in one way or another. Thus the rapes of Agnes Cole and Vicki are reminiscent of the sexual experiences of Cabot Wright and Pearl Miranda—one, a rapist; the other, victim of rape. In regard to similar occupations and incidents, we have Pearl, a schoolteacher, seeking refuge in the home of Warren Cramer, who is, like Agnes Cole, a piano teacher. Moreover, Pearl's naked journey through the streets can be compared to Winifred Fergus's walking out of the boardinghouse in her drawers. Again, Winifred, also a former schoolteacher who has never married, reminds us of Alma, the spinster schoolmarm of *The Nephew.*

The concept of writing to render a complete account is personified in Jeremy, and this in-depth presentation resembles the notebooks kept by Fenton Riddleway in which he recorded his ideas of the big city. Although Jeremy manages to record the full account of the Fergus-Summerland relationship through the early 1920s, we cannot help recalling such unsuccessful writers as Parkhearst Cratty in *63: Dream Palace* and the two Bickles in *Cabot Wright Begins*.

Money also plays a significant role in determining the motives of many of Purdy's characters; lack usually keeps his characters from living in any but a barren fashion. For example, the six thousand dollars that Rick inherits is akin to the four thousand dollars in *The Nephew* which Mrs. Barrington offers Vernon Miller so he can leave Rainbow Center. Vernon wishes to give this amount to Cliff, who, he thinks, needs to leave the confining influence of the town more than he himself does. This situation is analogous to Rick's in Boutflour, one in which his inheritance can be the means of his becoming an actor in New York.

In the instances in which characters desire, or possess, great wealth, we are reminded of analogous situations with Girard Girard in *Malcolm* and with Warburton in *Cabot Wright Begins*. In all cases, the desire for, or possession of, such riches is not a sure augury for happiness; in fact, it usually leads to the reverse. For example, Wilders Fergus turns out to be a philanderer, and is far from being either a good husband or father; Warburton commits suicide; Girard Girard ends his days lamenting his loneliness.

By far the most fascinating similarities of *Jeremy's Version* to its predecessors lie in those characters who eventually develop a hard-won wisdom, usually as a result of severe experience. Consequently, they know whereof they speak; and they are in a position to help those who have not as yet gained such an achievement. For example, Matt Brady, who is deeply disappointed that he has no father, is in a position to reassure Jeremy about one important matter: behind Jethro's desire to kill his mother lies the fact that "the fathomless love is disappointed love—it has all the rest of its life to bleed."[13] This statement also reminds us of Mrs. Barrington, who, once aware that she had to live her days with a husband who did not love her, is later in a position to understand better the nature of love. As a result, she is able to reassure Alma that Cliff, her nephew, had indeed loved his aunt and thus give the spinster great peace of mind.

As a clincher to certain similarities of incidents in Purdy's works, there is the letter which Jethro writes to the world to explain his reasons for wanting to kill his mother and, thus, his wish to start anew: this epistle can be compared to the clarifying missive Cabot Wright pens to Zoe Bickle as he "begins" to live his own life untrammeled by the past. All told, the sameness of themes, ideas, incidents, and attitudes in Purdy's fiction tends to become monotonous after a while. We hope, therefore, that Purdy will begin to realize this fact, since it is becoming increasingly evident that his tales of familial quarrels, orphaned children, and rape are beginning to become boring.

VI   *When   Last   Reviewed*

The reviews of *Jeremy's Version* have been mixed and are reminiscent of those of Purdy's previous works: of the first four reviews published, two were anything but enthusiastic; the other two were very complimentary. Guy Davenport found the scenes that Purdy had portrayed in the novel not new but nostalgic, an effect wonderfully exploited; however, Davenport also observed that *Jeremy's Version* was the kind of novel that has been written may times before by other writers. And, while the book was ostensibly about people who wanted to escape from one another and who wanted to wake up and live, the members of the Fergus family did not know what such living really entailed; instead, these characters reminded the reader of children on a rainy afternoon who want something but do not know exactly what they want.[14] On the other hand, Geoffrey Wolff's article was one of condemnation. Finding errors in the choice of language, such as *omniscient* for *omnivorous* reader, *nozzle* for *muzzle* of a gun, Wolff was almost malicious in his attack on the novel which he considered to have been written by an author who had an ear of "unalloyed tin" and who was writing in his latest opus the "turgid music of a soap opera." And, like the late Stanley Edgar Hyman, Wolff took issue with the deceased Dame Edith Sitwell's high evaluation of Purdy's talents, which he considered to be highly overrated.[15]

On the other hand, Burton L. Wimble thought Purdy's beginning work on the Fergus and Summerlad families an exciting one, for the novel made the reader eager to know what would be taking place in the other two works on the subject.

Purdy is, in fact, asserted Wimble, "one of the great technicians now writing in America"; and he recommended the book to all those interested in serious contemporary fiction.[16] An even more highly enthusiastic review was penned by James R. Lindroth, who thinks Purdy is both an excellent depicter of the appalling emotional difficulties involved in rearing a family, as well as one who has captured the quiet desperations of small-town life. Calling Purdy "one of the most talented novelists of the 1960's" Lindroth felt that in his new novel Purdy gave "promise to become one of the most significant voices of the seventies."[17] We cannot help agreeing with Lindroth that in *Jeremy's Version*, Purdy has produced one of his best novels to date, for the novel is a thoughtful portrayal of the ever mixed motives of men, women, and children; and it captures the sense of horror that lies close to what is considered to be normal. Moreover, Purdy is sure in his handling of character, incident, and theme. Last and most important, he leaves the reader at the end wanting to know more of the future doings of the Fergus family, a sure indication that he has made the reader "see" in the sense that Conrad meant the word to be understood.

CHAPTER 7

Purdy's Significance in Contemporary American Fiction

IN the three decades since the end of World War II, America has become the richest country in the world; at the same time a gradual deterioration in moral and spiritual values has taken place. As early as 1964, Purdy had written that "our moral life is pestiferous; we live in an immoral atmosphere." In the decade since then, corruption of the most blatant kind has become an everyday affair in our lives; it has been manifested, for example, in the highest level of government in the Watergate affair, and in big business in many instances. Again, while Purdy has never indicted organized religion as such (except for his misunderstanding of the teachings of Christian Science), a good many Americans would testify that the precepts set forth in the Mosaic Decalogue and in the Sermon on the Mount are fine ethical ideals but do not play a very significant role in determining or shaping the values in their lives.

Thus, in an age where secular leaders and religious faiths are found wanting in supplying inspiration or even leadership, a nation has to look to its writers for guidance and help. Just about one hundred and twenty-five years ago, Thomas Carlyle, John Ruskin, Matthew Arnold, and Charles Dickens, among others, were beginning to write some of their most important works, in their attempts to awaken their fellow Victorians to the need of raising their objectives and their thoughts to a higher level as the many problems of science, democracy, and nationalism bore down upon them. In a similar vein, Purdy can be classified with the great Victorians in that he has shown his fellow Americans in his fiction how horribly most of them have been living in the last generation. Like Carlyle, Purdy is a truth teller, a fact that has cost him dearly throughout his career, since various

125

publishers have repeatedly turned down his fiction because of its less than palatable themes.

In the three decades since the end of World War II—a period when American affluence and technological impersonality grew to astronomical heights and appeared to many Americans to be the be-all and end-all of human existence—Purdy dared to tell them the truth: behind the facade of great material wealth lay a vast spiritual wasteland of loveless lives and hellish marriages; from such barren marriages came children who, as a rule, were treated cruelly by their parents or by other adults; rape and homosexuality were engaged in by those who, denied love in their own lives, sought it in antisocial actions; and most ironic of all, the quest for wealth and the possession of it did not result in happiness.

That Purdy's fiction and the problems it portrays are as relevant for the 1970s as they were in the 1950s and 1960s can be seen in the fact that we cannot read a newspaper, a magazine, or a book these days without finding articles about any of the following topics: the viability of marriage and the family in the future; the cruelties inflicted on children by their parents or by other adults; the escalation in the number of rape victims; and the increasing clamor for civil rights by homosexuals. In fiction delineating such malaises, Purdy has resorted to shock devices, but certainly not for the sake of mere shock; rather, he has employed them, we think, to awaken his readers from the torpor into which many of them have fallen, lulled as they have been by the innumerable material satisfactions and pleasures easily available and by the ennui and boredom that accompany a surfeit of pleasures. If shock is effected by subject matter in which one homosexual is shown severing the genitals of another homosexual, or in which rape is as casually committed as the smoking of a cigarette, shock is not Purdy's purpose: he is intent upon showing us that these actions are simply the ugly results that occur in a society in which, despite a cornucopia of wealth and mountains of material goods, very little love is expressed by Americans for one another. Indeed, a person in Purdy's fiction does not so much die of love as he does from a lack or betrayal of this life-giving and life-animating quality; therefore, the lack of love in the lives of those so affected leads them to seek love in what would be considered antisocial actions. Still, Purdy's forte is not his choice of subject matter and its shock effect, for all of us know that shocks resident in subject matter soon cease to be effective; it is rather in the shock of style that Purdy excels. For, in narrating his tales of blighted lives, he manages to portray scenes in which the extremely abnormal is linked to the so-called normal in ways that have a degree of verisimilitude not previously thought of; in which unexpected aspects of character surface when least expected; in which the lovelessness of modern marriages is set forth in a minimum of dialogue but with such vividness and horror that the reader knows instinctively that he has never before experienced these terrors in print.

This shock of style never ceases to be effective and startling and applies to practically all of his fiction, with *63: Dream Palace*, "Color of Darkness," and "Daddy Wolf" as immediate examples. This power is seen in the use of such technical devices as jostling contradictions, the mixing of the banal and the wise, the juxtaposition of the grotesque and the normal—all in absolutely new ways. In fact, Purdy's major strength lies in his ability to take so-called repellent subject matter and so work with it that he turns it into a true work of art, much like the ugly driftwood which undergoes a change into something rich and strange when worked upon by a master. All this is accomplished in a style that is not only unique in its simplicity, but which is also characterized by clarity, force and beauty—the three chief qualities of good writing. In addition to Purdy's ability to write unforgettable parables of the way Americans have lived in the past two decades, Purdy's loveless view of life is rich in humor of various kinds—zany, "black," surreal or quietly reflective. We all remember how the drunken porter's humor in Shakespeare's *Macbeth* serves as a contrast to Duncan's murder; as a result, this swinish humor helps set this ghastly deed in stark relief. In Purdy's case, his humor does not serve as a contrast to the dour actions that he usually narrates; instead, his humor is warp and woof of his style; and an example of the humor of the quietly reflective kind illustrates this point. In "Plan Now To Attend," the reader notes that Fred, who normally drinks heavily to bury his sense of emptiness, is shown listening very carefully and soberly to his friend Ezra Hightower, the converted atheist, who is muttering in his drunken stupor that Fred will ultimately be saved. Such a scene reveals Purdy's ability to intertwine aspects of humor with the elements of tragedy but to keep uppermost the tragic sense.

Purdy's talent is a many-sided one; for, in addition to being an instinctive portrayer of the dark underside of human nature, he is also an excellent regionalist, as is seen in *The Nephew* and a crack fantasist, as in *Malcolm*. Purdy's ability as a satirist has already been dwelt upon in *Cabot Wright Begins*, but *Eustace Chisholm and The Works* reveals his strength as a Realist who depicts the tragic world of homosexuality. But Purdy has, in fact, created many worlds; and each with its own discernible and distinct features. Each of these worlds is populated with a host of characters: orphans, thoughtless and cruel parents, failed artists, budding writers and actors, spinsters, grand ladies, teachers and professors, widowers and widows, financiers, homosexuals, and invalids—all of whom form a veritable gallery of typical figures of and for our time. That these characters deeply affected and influenced his portrayal of them, Purdy made clear when he told an interviewer, "My biography is my books. Just say I tried to write about what I knew and felt in my American tongue."[1]

However much Purdy has been on target in depicting the malaises of contemporary society, and however faithfully and stylistically he delineates these problems, his portrait of contemporary America nonetheless lacks balance in certain respects. First, not a single character in his fiction can be said to be a truly happy person, in the sense that the character's potentialities have to a degree been fulfilled. Second, no Jews are presented in his works—a glaring omission in an age when these people have played such important roles in American life and have also filled the pages of so many contemporary novelists. Third, there is a scarcity of good people in his fiction—people who would perform an unselfish act merely for the pleasure such an act would provide. Fourth—and here Purdy can be scored—there are many marriages that are really a union of hearts, and there are the children of these marriages who grow up to become loving parents themselves. Fifth, in his humor, an area where

Purdy excels, never once do we find a play of wit; this omission
is probably due to the lack of intellectuals in his works.

Because of his consistently dour vision, we would say that
Purdy has an affinity with the Naturalists. But where such earlier
writers as Theodore Dreiser, James Farrell, and John Dos Passos
fashioned characters who were shown as scrambling for survival
and buffeted by an indifferent universe, Purdy's characters, on
the other hand, are not so circumstanced. Rather, their emotional
deficiences—their inability to give or receive love in any meaningful way—subjects them to our careful scrutiny and finally
arouses our compassion for their disability.

An interview Purdy held with Barton Midwood in October,
1970, shortly after the publication of *Jeremy's Version*, clarified
one of the conspicuous omissions in his fiction—the absence of
Jewish characters. Purdy admitted quite candidly that anti-
Semitism constituted a major problem for him.[2] In the same
interview, Purdy, who still has hang-ups about the publishing
business, complained about the New York literary establishment and the fact that the Sunday *New York Times Book Review* was chiefly concerned "with fashions and tricks." Yet on
June 6, 1971, Purdy (along with Peter DeVries, Frank Conroy,
Anthony Burgess, and Richard Brautigan, among others) was
enlisted by the *Times* to write articles playing up the art of
parody.

Purdy's attempt hilariously burlesqued the manner in which
books, say those of a Jacqueline Susann, get written, are quickly
made into movies, and just as quickly make writers and the
Hollywood producers associated with them millionaires. The
heroine of the parody, "Boogie Boome in the Big Time," is a
girl who "had a mud fence for a face." She works in a big plastic
hospital and later is highly successful with her biography, "From
Bandages to Bandwagon." Pushed by Attar Wimminsure, the
Hollywood mogul, with the help of Robin Useto, "a big down-
town editor who was getting ready to go uptown," Boogie's
entire biography was found to have such sex appeal as to be
given royal treatment "in the world's bulkiest book section
spread," what else but the *New York Times*.[3]

In conclusion, we could forecast Purdy's future as a writer to
be a promising one; however, he is at a crucial point in his career.

Should he continue to write about orphans, failed and miserable marriages, rape, and homosexuality, readers will soon conclude that Purdy has run out of material for his fiction. On the other hand, should he grow and use new and different source material for his fiction, readers will eagerly seek to see what a fundamentally honest craftsman has fashioned that is fresh. Living in New York, one of the most exciting cities in the world, it is inconceivable that Purdy—aware of the successes of such books as Saul Bellow's *Mr. Sammler's Planet* and Bernard Malamud's *The Tenants*—will not also use this metropolis of more than eight million people as basic literary ore for his future fiction. Should he, however, not develop new themes but adhere to his former ones, he will still remain important as an author who wrote about Americans and the way they were in the 1950s and the 1960s. With his many characters who suffer so deeply and lamentably because of a lack or betrayal of love, Purdy has fashioned several works of art out of the dark interiors of the human soul. With his satirical treatment of many aspects of American life, he has portrayed a way of life, which apparently is materially successful, but at rock bottom is characterized in many instances by spiritual bankruptcy and has caused us many of our current problems.

All told, Purdy is a writer of marvelous power, who has made us think deeply and seriously about the human condition, which he regards woefully. At the same time, his style, based as a good deal of it is on the speech of his native Ohio, delights us and reminds us of Twain's, whose books are filled with the many varieties of speech engaged in by antebellum Missourians living along the Mississippi River. In short, Purdy's power and style are two positive virtues in a period when many writers simply lack one or another of these ingredients in their works.

Notes and References

Preface

1. Introduction, *Color of Darkness*, Lippincott ed. (New York, 1957), p. 9.
2. Stanley Edgar Hyman, *Standards: A Chronicle of Books for Our Time* (New York, 1966), p. 254.

Chapter One

1. William Peden, *The American Short Story: Front Line in the National Defense of Literature* (Boston, 1964), p. 91 n.
2. From a letter dated January 18, 1966, to the author from James Purdy. Hereafter referred to as "Letter."
3. From autobiographical material sent to Wilson Company, New York, to be included in *World Authors*, 1950–1970.
4. Evelyn Geller, "WLB Biography: James Purdy," *Wilson Library Bulletin* (March, 1964), pp. 572–74.
5. See footnote 3 above.
6. John W. Aldridge, *Time to Murder and Create: The Contemporary Novel in Crisis* (New York, 1966), XI.
7. Richard Chase, *The American Novel and Its Tradition* (New York, 1957), IX.
8. Nathalie Sarraute, *New York Times Book Review*, April 24, 1966, p. 2.
9. *The Nephew*, Farrar, Straus ed. (New York, 1960), p. 13.
10. Gerald Weales, "No Face and No Exit: The Fiction of James Purdy and J. P. Donleavy," in *Contemporary American Novelists* (Carbondale, Ill., 1964), p. 149.

Chapter Two

1. William Peden, "And Never a Silver Lining," *New York Times Book Review*, December 29, 1957, p. 4.
2. "Color of Darkness," *New York Herald Tribune Book Review*, December 29, 1957, p. 3.

131

3. As recently as 1964, Purdy complained of critics and reviewers whose influence has prevented his fiction from being published by various publishers.

4. *"Color of Darkness,"* Lippincott, ed. (New York, 1957), p. 29.

5. Ibid., "Why Can't They Tell You Why?" p. 65.

6. Ibid., "Cutting Edge," p. 124.

7. Ibid., "Eventide," p. 58.

8. Ibid., "Don't Call Me by My Right Name," p. 47.

9. Ibid., "Man and Wife," p. 76.

10. Ibid., "Sound of Talking," p. 114.

11. Ibid., "You Reach for Your Hat," p. 86.

12. Ibid., "A Good Woman," p. 97.

13. Ibid., "You May Safely Gaze," p. 39.

14. Ibid., "Plan Now to Attend," p. 105.

15. "The State of the Story," *Nation,* CLXXXVI (January 11, 1958), 35.

16. Introduction, *Color of Darkness,* op. cit., p. 12.

17. "Reading Your Own," *New York Times Book Review,* June 4, 1967, p. 32.

18. Quoted in Introduction, *Color of Darkness,* op. cit., p. 10.

Chapter Three

1. Donald Cook, "By the World Possessed," *New Republic,* CXLI (November 9, 1959), 26.

2. Introduction, *Malcolm* (New York, 1959), p. IX.

3. Granville Hicks, "Purdy, Humes, Ellis," *Saturday Review,* XLII (September 26, 1959), 15.

4. Thomas F. Curley, "The Sleep-Walker," *Commonweal,* LXXI (October 16, 1959), 80.

5. Whitney Balliett, "Underseas with Purdy and Humes," *New Yorker,* XXXV (December 19, 1959), 138–39.

6. *Malcolm,* Farrar, Straus ed. (New York, 1959), p. 9.

7. Ibid., p. 149.

8. Ibid., p. 108.

9. Ibid., p. 207.

10. Ibid., p. 98.

11. Ibid., p. 114.

12. Ibid., p. 104.

13. Richard Foster, "What Is Fiction For?" *Hudson Review Quarterly,* XIV (Spring, 1961), 142.

14. William Peden, "Mystery of the Missing Kin," *Saturday Review,* XLIII (November 26, 1960), 22.

15. *The Nephew*, Farrar, Straus ed. (New York, 1960). Clara Himbaugh had had some teeth extracted without an anesthetic. Had not Alma Mason visited her at the right time, the woman would have died from the excruciating pain.
16. Ibid., "Yes, Cliff loved you," p. 208.
17. Ibid., p. 176.
18. Ibid., p. 141.

Chapter Four

1. *Children Is All*, New Directions ed. (New York, 1961). Seven of the stories had appeared during the period from 1957–1961 in the following magazines: *Commentary, Esquire, New Directions 17, New World Writing 17, Partisan Review*, and *The Texas Quarterly*.
2. Ibid., "Mrs. Benson," p. 77.
3. Ibid., "About Jessie Mae," p. 34.
4. Ibid., "Home by Dark," pp. 22–23.
   Ibid., p. 00.
5. Ibid., "Night and Day," p. 67.
6. Ibid., "Daddy Wolf," p. 5.
7. Ibid., "Everything Under the Sun," p. 89.
8. Ibid., "Encore," p. 50.
9. Ibid., "The Lesson," p. 45.
10. Ibid., "Goodnight, Sweetheart," p. 108.
11. Ibid., "Sermon," p. 82.
12. Ibid., "Cracks," p. 169.
13. Ibid., p. 157.
14. Lewis Funke, *New York Times*, October 1, 1963, p. 34.
15. Ihab Hassan, "Of Anguish and Incongruity," *Saturday Review*, XLV (November 17, 1962), 49.
16. W. T. Scott, "The Zephyrs of Death," *New Republic*, CXLVII (November 17, 1962), 25.
17. William Peden, "Out of Contrasts Two Fictional Worlds," *Virginia Quarterly*, XXXIX (Spring, 1963), 4.
18. Benjamin DeMott, "The New Books," *Harper*, CCXXVI (January, 1963), 91.
19. Guy Davenport, "Three Miscellanies," *National Review*, XIV (February 26, 1963), 162.
20. Robert Taubman, "Clerical Errors," *New Statesman*, LXVI (August 16, 1963), 199.
21. Irving Malin, "Occasions for Loving," *Kenyon Review*, XXV (Spring, 1963), 348.

Chapter Five

1. "Works in Progress, 1963," *Esquire* (July, 1963), p. 51.
2. *Cabot Wright Begins*, Farrar, Straus ed. (New York, 1964), p. 4.
3. Ibid., p. 139.
4. Ibid., p. 184.
5. Ibid., p. 171.
6. Ibid., pp. 100–101.
7. Ibid., p. 172.
8. Frederick Crews, "Private Lives, Public Lives," *New York Review of Books*, III (November 5, 1964), p. 13.
9. *Cabot Wright Begins*, op. cit., p. 174.
10. Ibid., p. 206.
11. Ibid., p. 209. *Buttercup*, of course, rhymes with *moneycup*.
12. Ibid., p. 149.
13. Ibid., pp. 211–12.
14. Ibid., p. 164.
15. Ibid., p. 199.
16. Ibid., p. 29.
17. Ibid., p. 203.
18. Ibid., p. 201.
19. Ibid., p. 203.
20. Orville Prescott, "The Waste of a Small Talent," *New York Times Book Review*, October 19, 1964, p. 31.
21. *Cabot Wright Begins*, op. cit., p. 158.
22. Ibid., p. 192.
23. Ibid., p. 96.
24. Ibid., p. 213.
25. Stanley Edgar Hyman, "The Correction of Opinion (James Purdy)," *New Leader*, XIX (November 23, 1964), 449.
26. Theodore Solotaroff, "The Deadly James Purdy," *New York Herald Tribune Book Week*, October 18, 1964, p. 44.
27. Eric Moon, *Library Journal*, LXXXIX (October 15, 1964), 3973.
28. *Eustace Chisholm and The Works* (New York, 1967), p. 81.
29. Ibid., p. 81.
30. Ibid., p. 85.
31. Ibid., p. 208.
32. Ibid., pp. 204–5.
33. Ibid., p. 115.
34. Ibid., pp. 233–34.

35. Wilfrid Sheed, "An Alleged Love Story," *New York Times Book Review*, May 21, 1967, p. 4.

36. Angus Wilson, "Purdy Pushes Comedy Past Blackness," *Life Book Review*, June 2, 1967, p. 8.

37. Irving Malin, "Eustace Chisholm and The Works," *Commonweal*, LXXXVI (July 28, 1967), 476–77.

38. Ross Wetzsteon, "Making It the Hard Way," *Washington Post Book Week*, May 28, 1967, p. 4.

39. Richard K. Morris, "James Purdy and the Works," *Nation*, CCX (October 9, 1967), 342–44.

40. Barry Gross, "Pseudo-Poet and -Man," *Saturday Review*, L (August 5, 1967), 37–38.

41. Warren Coffey, "The Incomplete Novelist," *Commentary* (September, 1967), 98–103.

Chapter Six

1. *New York Times Book Review*, October 11, 1970, p. 11.

2. *Jeremy's Version*, (New York, 1970), p. 112.

3. Ibid., p. 53.

4. Ibid., p. 162.

5. Ibid., p. 158.

6. Ibid., p. 126.

7. Ibid., p. 208.

8. Ibid., p. 89.

9. Ibid., p. 84.

10. Ibid., pp. 251–52.

11. Ibid., p. 233.

12. Ibid., p. 263.

13. Ibid., p. 263.

14. Guy Davenport, "Jeremy's Version," *New York Times Book Review*, November 15, 1970, p. 4.

15. Geoffrey Wolff, *Newsweek*, LXXVI (October 12, 1970), p. 122.

16. Burton L. Wimble, *Library Journal*, LXLVI (October 1, 1970), 3306.

17. James R. Lindroth, *America*, CXXIV (February 27, 1971), 211.

Chapter Seven

1. Gordon Lish, *New Sounds in American Fiction* (Menlo Park, California, 1969), p. 110.

2. Barton Midwood, "Short Visits with Five Writers and One Friend," *Esquire* (November, 1970), 150–51.

3. James Purdy, "Success Story," *New York Times Book Review*, June 6, 1971, pp. 24, 26.

Selected Bibliography

PRIMARY SOURCES

All the published works of James Purdy are listed chronologically.

1. Books

Color of Darkness. New York: J. B. Lippincott Company, 1957.
Malcolm. New York: Farrar, Straus and Company, 1959.
The Nephew. New York: Avon Books, 1962.
Children Is All. New York: New Directions, 1961.
Cabot Wright Begins. New York: Farrar, Straus and Giroux, 1964.
Eustace Chisholm and The Works. New York: Farrar, Straus and Giroux, 1967.
Jeremy's Version. New York: Doubleday and Company, 1970.

2. Paperback editions

Color of Darkness and *Children Is All.* New York: Avon Books, 1965.
Malcolm. New York: Avon Books, 1960.
The Nephew. New York: Avon Books, 1965.
Cabot Wright Begins. New York: Avon Books, 1965.

3. Some anthologies in which Purdy's stories appear.

Cleanth Brooks and Robert Penn Warren. *Understanding Fiction.* "Eventide." New York: Appleton-Century-Crofts, 1959.
Bruce Jay Friedman, ed. *Black Humor.* "Don't Call Me By My Right Name." New York: Bantam Books, 1965.
Richard Kostelanetz. *12 From the Sixties.* "Goodnight Sweetheart." New York: Dell Publishing Company, 1967.
Gordon Lish, ed. *New Sounds in American Fiction.* "Daddy Wolf." Menlo Park, Calif.: Cummings Publishing Company, 1969.

SECONDARY SOURCES

1. Biographical Material

Evelyn Geller. "WLB: Biography: James Purdy." *Wilson Library Bulletin* (March, 1964), pp. 572, 574. Autobiographical material sent author, which had been previously sent to the Wilson Company for inclusion in *World Authors* 1950–1970.

2. Criticism of Purdy's Works

ALDRIDGE, JOHN W. *Time to Murder and Create: The Contemporary Novel in Crisis.* New York: David McKay Co., 1966. Purdy is included among a developing group of serious younger writers such as Salinger, Bellow, Malamud, Roth, Herbert Gold, and the late Flannery O'Connor, all of whom are seen "as minting a fresh currency of the creative imagination."

BALDANZA, FRANK. "Playing House for Keeps with James Purdy." *Wisconsin Studies in Contemporary Literature,* II (Autumn, 1970), 489–510. Fine analysis of the novels, which are viewed as studies of family life; the orphans are almost always treated as "the insulted and the injured" and receive all the abuse and torment this denotes.

BURGESS, ANTHONY. *The Novel Now: A Guide to Contemporary Fiction.* New York: W. W. Norton & Co., 1967. The country of the self viewed as the theme of much of Purdy's work.

BURRIS, SHIRLEY W. "The Emergency in Purdy's 'Daddy Wolf.'" *Renascence,* XX (Winter, 1968), 94–98, 103. In a world where the helpfulness of religion is not apparent, the telephone becomes an important means of communication.

COFFEY, WARREN. "The Incompleat Novelist: Eustace Chisholm and The Works." *Commentary* (September, 1967), 37–38. In his ever-recurring theme of "lost childhood," Purdy is guilty of not having forgotten or forgiven his own lost days as a child.

COTT, JONATHAN. "The Damaged Cosmos." *On Contemporary Literature.* Edited by Richard Kostelanetz. New York: Avon Book Division, 1964. The purposeless nature of the modern world as revealed in *Malcolm* is inherent in the nature of things, since the cosmos itself is damaged.

DAICHES, DAVID. "Malcolm." *Antioch Review,* XXII (Spring, 1962), 122–30. Daiches regards the book as a very funny one expressing "the delight of truly original comedy."

DENNISTON, CONSTANCE. "The American Romance-Parody: A Study of Purdy's *Malcolm* and Heller's *Catch-22.*" *Emporia State Research Studies,* XIV, 2 (1965), 42–59, 63–64. The romance, which usually ends with the elevation of the hero, reverses itself in both works, and is thus parodied.

FIEDLER, LESLIE A. *The Return of the Vanishing American.* New York: Stein and Day, 1968. Color is no bar in the expression of love, even if it is of a homosexual nature as in the Bernie Glad-hart–Winters Hart relationship in *Cabot Wright Begins.*

FINKELSTEIN, SIDNEY. *Existentialism and Alienation in American Literature.* New York: International Publishers, 1965. Purdy seen as having assumed the stance of alienation as a matter of fact and having disciplined himself "to tell nothing, to be affected by nothing. . . ."

FRENCH, WARREN. "The Quaking World of James Purdy." *Essays in Modern American Literature.* Edited by Richard E. Langford. Stetson, Florida: Stetson University Press, 1963. "Quaking" in the sense that the world today seems about ready to fragment into a million meaningless pieces, all because of the hostility in it.

HASSAN, IHAB. *Radical Innocence: Studies in The Contemporary American Novel.* New York: Harper and Row, 1961. Good discussion of the child in our society who is eternally victimized by the conflict within himself and the society in which he lives. Applies specifically to Claire in *63: Dream Palace.*

————. "Laughter in the Dark: The New Voice in American Fiction." *American Scholar,* XXXIII (Autumn, 1964), 636–39. Variety of comedic responses are made to the absurdity and horror of modern life. Like Carson McCullers, Purdy uses laughter to describe spiritual distortion.

————. "The Dial and Recent American Fiction." *Critic,* I (October, 1966), 3. Discusses the different kinds of novels written in the last decade, such as the slapstick, neo-picaresque, ironic, as well as the novel of outrage and the Gothic. Purdy's works are placed among the last type.

HERR, PAUL. "The Small, Sad World of James Purdy." *Chicago Review,* XIV (Autumn–Winter, 1960), 19–25. Claims Purdy's world is very close to the truth of American life in our time.

HORCHLER, RICHARD. "Impending Revelations." *Commonweal,* LXXVII (January 4, 1963), 393–400. The inconsequential is charged with the unbearable weight of significance in Purdy's fiction.

HYMAN, STANLEY EDGAR. "The Correction of Opinion (James Purdy)." *Standards: A Chronicle of Books for Our Time.* New York: Horizon Press, 1966. Hyman consideres Purdy to be vastly overrated.

KOSTELANETZ, RICHARD. "The New American Fiction." *The New American Arts.* Edited by Richard Kostelanetz. New York: Collier Books, 1965. Purdy classified with Barth, Heller, and Pynchon as seeing the world as essentially absurd and as constructing fiction to fit this view.

LEWIS, R. W. B. "Recent Fiction: Picaro and Pilgrim." *A Time of Harvest*. Edited by Robert E. Spiller. New York: Hill and Wang, 1962. In its rejection of much of contemporary life, *Malcolm* is shown exploring significant aspects of this life.

LORCH, THOMAS M. "Purdy's *Malcolm*: A Unique Vision of Radical Emptiness." *Wisconsin Studies in Contemporary Literature*, VI (Summer, 1965), 204–13. A world of terrifying emptiness is portrayed in which all familiar logic and meaning have been perverted and destroyed.

LUDWIG, JACK. *Recent American Novelists*. American Writers, 22. Minneapolis: University of Minnesota Press, 1962. Homosexuality as a form of communion is shown as emerging from the new American courtly love tradition, albeit grotesquely, in *Malcolm* and *The Nephew*.

MALIN, IRVING. *New American Gothic*. Carbondale: Southern Illinois University Press, 1964. The family is portrayed as an essentially destructive element, an attitude adhered to in the novels of Hawkes, McCullers, Salinger, and Purdy.

MALOFF, SAUL. "James Purdy's Fictions: The Quality of Despair." *Critique*, VI (Spring, 1963), 106–12. The despair that characterizes much of Purdy's fiction derives from a loveless world.

MILLER, JAMES E. *Quests Surd and Absurd*. Chicago: University of Chicago Press, 1967. Purdy placed in the cultist group along with Hawkes and Terry Southern in Miller's view of current American novelists.

O'CONNOR, WILLIAM VAN. "The Grotesque: An American Genre." *The Grotesque*. Edited by William Van O'Connor. Carbondale: Southern Illinois University Press, 1962. The grotesque treated as a peculiarly American literary genre with the characters so labeled unable to communicate and express affection.

PEDEN, WILLIAM. *The American Short Story: Front Line in the National Defense of Literature*. Boston: Houghton Mifflin Co., 1964. Along with Capote and Flannery O'Connor, Purdy is treated as one of the more significant writers about the abnormal.

POMERANZ, REGINA. "The Hell of Not Loving: Purdy's Modern Tragedy." *Renascence* (Spring, 1964), pp. 149–53. Loss of self and human identity are central themes of Purdy's fiction.

SCHWARSCHILD, BETTINA. "The Forsaken: An Interpretive Essay on James Purdy's Malcolm." *Texas Quarterly*, X, 1 (Spring, 1967), 170–77. Malcolm is not shown as going off on a quest for a greater sense of life, but to his death.

————. "Aunt Alma: James Purdy's The Nephew." *University of Windsor Review*, III (Fall, 1967), 80–87. Alma gets to know herself better only as a result of coming into contact with her neighbors.

SKERRETT, TAYLOR, JR. "Dostoyevsky, Nathaniel West and Some Contemporary Fiction." *University of Dayton Review*, IV, i (1966), 23–35. Claims the black humor of such writers as Heller, Bruce Jay Friedman, and Purdy originates in Sterne, Fielding, Dostoyevsky and the pessimism originates in Twain and West.

————. "James Purdy and the Works: Love and Tragedy in Five Novels." *Twentieth Century Literature*, XV (April, 1969), 25–53. Lack of love in one way or another leads to tragedy in all five works.

SCHOTT, WEBSTER. "James Purdy: American Dreams." *Nation*, CXCVIII (March 23, 1964), 300–303. Purdy has a vision of a dead and decaying society and is writing in sorrow over the corpse.

SOLOTAROFF, THEODORE. "The Deadly James Purdy." *The Red Hot Vacuum*. New York: Atheneum, 1970. Purdy's fiction fulfills Ezra Pound's dictum "Make it new."

STRAUMANN, HEINRICH. *American Literature in the Twentieth Century*. 3rd rev. ed. New York: Harper and Row, 1966. Purdy classified with John Updike, since much of their fiction is concerned with young people and the manner in which life impinges upon them.

WAGER, WILLIS. *American Literature: A World View*. New York: New York University Press, 1968. Purdy's black humor drawn not only from American but also from Continental roots.

WEALES, GERALD. "No Face and No Exit: The Fiction of James Purdy and J. P. Donleavy." *Contemporary American Novelists*. Edited by Harry T. Moore. Carbondale: Southern Illinois University Press, 1964. Purdy's heroes have no faces except the ones reflected in the eyes of others, as contrasted with Donleavy's, who have a multitude of faces and disguises that they assume to protect themselves from an unfriendly world.

WEST, PAUL. *The Modern Novel: The United States and Other Countries*. Vol. II. London: Hutchinson University Library, 1963. Purdy's fiction viewed as an account of the unclassifiable mysteries beneath the conventional surfaces.

Index

(The works of Purdy are listed under his name)

142

DATE			